THE WOW FACTOR

*How I Turned One Great Idea and
My Unbridled Enthusiasm into a Golf
Revolution*

Barney Adams

SKYHORSE PUBLISHING

To my mother, Bertha Beckwith Adams, who at ninety-two is my inspiration, but really no more so than she has been all my life. Through her, to my dad, William Adams, gone these many years but not forgotten.

And to Jim Marshall, who passed before this book was finished. He was my dear friend, my mentor, and I hope this effort is worthy of the good advice he gave me.

Finally, to my wife Jackie, and Cindy, Eddie, and Susan.

Skyhorse Publishing books may be purchased in bulk at special discounts for sales promotion, corporate gifts, fund raising, or educational purposes. Special editions can also be created to specifications. For details, contact Special Sales Department, Skyhorse Publishing, 555 Eighth Avenue, Suite 903, New York, NY 10018 or info@skyhorsepublishing.com.

www.skyhorsepublishing.com

Library of Congress Cataloging-in-Publication Data
    Adams, Barney.
    The wow factor : how I turned one great idea and my unbridled enthusiasm
        into a golf revolution / Barney Adams.
        p.   cm.
    Includes index.
    ISBN 978-1-60239-248-9
    1. Adams, Barney. 2. Golf equipment industry—United States.
    3. Businessmen--United States—Biography. I. Title.
    HD9993.G652A33 A3 2008
    338.7'68876352092—dc22
    [B]

                                2008013387

10 9 8 7 6 5 4 3 2 1

Printed in the United States of America

CONTENTS

Part Two: Inside the Golf Equipment Industry

FOREWORD

Tales From the Barnyard

I first met Barney Adams when he responded to my monthly column in American Express's flagship travel magazine regarding the esoteric subject of club fitting. The year was 1996.

A certain major equipment company that shall go unnamed had taken exception to my assertion that the clubs I'd had "custom-made" and purchased at full retail price from them simply didn't perform the way I'd hoped and expected them to. Furthermore, I stated that I wasn't convinced there was a whole lot to the custom-fitting craze then sweeping the consumer golf equipment industry. Last, I made a lighthearted joke about the staggering price of drivers and fairway woods that manufacturers were suddenly commanding being proportionate to the difficulty of using them to hit in actual playing circumstances.

In his friendly letter, Barney pointed out that much of what passes for serious club-fitting in many instances was simply a marketing ploy intended make the paying customer feel like he'd purchased the ideal set of golf clubs based on a few simple physical calculations. "Real club-fitting takes place the only place it can," he wrote. "On the golf course or the practice range." He graciously invited me to hop a plane to Plano, Texas, and tour his plant at Adams Golf, whereupon he would personally check out the specs on my new under-performing custom-made sticks and give me an honest analysis. Unknown to me then was the fact that Barney Adams was one of the true innovators and modern pioneers of custom-fitting.

"As for the overpriced, under-performing fairway woods," he added. "I'd love to show you something we've developed that just may change your thinking on the subject."

I decided to accept his invitation—if only to get a colorful column from the experience.

Picking me up at the airport in Dallas, Barney whisked me out to Hank Haney's Golf Ranch and put me through an extensive club-fitting examination on a lie board and on the range. My expensive new under-performing clubs turned out to be woefully misfit—two-degree upright, among other things, for a swing that was three-degree flat, hence my propensity to hit soaring hooks.

Adams offered to make a new set that properly matched my swing specs, and placed an odd-looking reverse trapezoidal fairway wood in my hands, inviting me to give it a swing. The club had recently been introduced and was about to be marketed, interestingly enough, through a series of infomercials featuring the club-maker himself.

For the next twenty minutes, I stood on the Haney range nailing one beautiful shot after the other to the back of the range.

"Holy cow," I finally said, noting the ease with which this odd-looking fairway wood got the ball airborne off the turf. "What *is* this thing?"

"We call it the Tight Lies. And that's 'WOW factor, by the way,'" my host allowed. "It's the key to everything we try to do around here at Adams Golf. If it doesn't WOW, it doesn't work."

Over the next two days, I learned a lot about Barney Adams and the hard science behind the amazing Tight Lies fairway wood, which would soon become the best-selling fairway club in golf and spawn a host of expensive copycat clubs across the industry-at-large.

Looking back, it's fair to say this novel fairway club had the same kind of revolutionary effect on making the game easier to play for millions of golfers of all skill levels that perimeter-weighted clubs and oversized metal drivers had on the game of golf.

Some years later, while sitting in on a major panel discussion about the evolution of golf equipment and the effects of exploding technology on the direction of the game, I was asked by a reporter if I could name the four or five greatest advances in equipment technology in the past half century.

"That's easy," I said, and ticked off Karsten Solheim's development of perimeter-weighting technology in putters, Gary Adams's development of metal drivers, Ely Callaway's refinement of metal driver technology in the Big Bertha, and Barney Adams's creation of the Tight Lies fairway wood. In my judgment, I said, these were the true modern equipment pioneers of the game of golf.

What I didn't tell the reporter was that I'd had the opportunity to get to know three of the aforementioned legends pretty well, including Ely Callaway and both Adamses (who share a surname but aren't related). Callaway, in fact, had recently taken me to dinner at his club in Southern California and floated the idea of my helping him write a book about the creation of Big Bertha. During the evening's discussions, the subject of his industry competitors came up. Callaway smiled wryly and observed, "You know, if I was half as smart as some people say I am, I would try to buy Adams Golf and hire Barney Adams to lead Callaway Golf into the future." Ely admitted he was a huge admirer of the Tight Lies fairway wood and other Adams creations and was pretty clear that the relationship was something he definitely planned to explore.

I couldn't disagree with his logic. Since that first encounter at the Hank Haney Ranch, I'd gotten to know Barney Adams on both a professional and personal basis and found him to be one of the most refreshingly honest and brilliant thinkers I'd ever met—an engagingly rumpled scientist-turned-businessman who literally sketched up the future on a pad of paper and made it happen.

"Barnyard" Adams's marketing moxie was evident in his groundbreaking infomercials, as well. First and last, Callaway was a marketing genius who understood the buying public's instinctive desire to find a golf club that simply made the act of hitting a golf ball where you wanted it to go easier and therefore more enjoyable—exactly the same effect Adams produced with his WOW factor and the Tight Lies fairway woods. The two men shared a nearly identical mission in life.

Not long after my dinner with Ely, Arnold Palmer asked me to help him write his memoirs and Ely Callaway fully understood my desire to help the King of Golf translate his oversized life to the page. Callaway eventually hired another writer to take on the task of telling the tale of Big Bertha but, alas, passed away before the project could be completed.

To make matters worse, Gary Adams and Karsten Solheim also passed away about this same time, leaving great stories of their pioneering roles in creating the modern equipment revolution untold and perhaps eventually forgotten.

Fortunately there is one legend still alive and very much kicking, a big rumpled barnyard character with a load of fabulous insights and refreshingly honest tales to tell from deep inside the golf equipment revolution he helped create.

In my opinion, nobody knows more than Barney Adams about how far the equipment business has come from the first steel shafts of the 1930s to the oversized space-age technologies of today—and about where things may be headed from here.

The WOW factor Barney Adams created and personifies is colorfully revealed in the pages of this engaging memoir, written by the man who helped create the revolution.

I know you'll find these industry insider tales from the Barnyard to be both entertaining and deeply illuminating—as fun to read as his legendary Tight Lies is to play.

Enjoy.

—James Dodson
Author of *Final Rounds* and *Ben Hogan: An American Life*

INTRODUCTION

*W*hether during talks or casual conversations, after hearing the story of Adams Golf countless people have told me that I should write a book about my experiences. Like anyone who would undertake such a project, I first tried to formulate the book in my head. What would it be like? What was my goal? And, more important, how could it be an enjoyable reading experience? Researching the business-book sections of bookstores, I came upon two general approaches, but neither seemed to fit. In the first approach, the book established a management system. The author would follow the book, I'm sure, with speaking engagements and a CD, all packaged at an attractive price.

I could also have gone for the "managerial brilliance" approach—hiring a ghostwriter to review my career and find enough flashes of insight, combined with some creative writing, to do the trick.

Upon further review, however, I determined that this approach would have produced a book approximately seventeen pages in length. And that assumes a liberal use of adjectives and some clever writing, combined with my (very) selective memory.

I've given many speeches, and found that they were a useful vehicle to tell my story. That's the style I've chosen to use with this book. It's about telling a story and offering some advice where applicable, not about selling a management system.

I also struggled with the title. My choice was something incredibly creative like *The Adams Golf Story*. The good folks at Skyhorse Publishing convinced me that *The WOW Factor* was a much more marketable approach, and the inner Barnyard said, "Yes, you dope, it's about sales."

The new name did create a problem for me, though, because I figured if *The WOW Factor* were the title, I should introduce the concept early in the book and refer back to it as a repeating theme, like in a classical symphony. The only problem is that this is a true story, and telling it in sequence means WOW shows up when it actually happened, which is well into the book. Any attempt to introduce it earlier would be fabricated because I certainly wasn't aware of the phenomenon until it happened. That doesn't mean it isn't important; in fact, it not only kept me going through some tough times, it's also a philosophy I believe is applicable to any business. So while I agree that WOW makes for a good title, it will be part and parcel of the Adams Golf story, exactly as it occurred.

It dawned on me that as much as I believed in WOW, it might be a good idea to see if it had credibility in the scientific world. For this, I contacted my close friend, Dr. Richard Coop, a sports psychologist and retired professor from the University of North Carolina, with whom I share an interest in rooting for the Tarheels basketball program. "Dr. C" always looks forward to my calls because of my incredible insight into basketball and, most specifically, the field of psychology.

When I asked Dr. C about WOW, he agreed that it had significant value and slowly, using carefully selected words, explained to me the field of the adaptive unconscious. He referenced *Blink*, a popular book by Malcom Gladwell, which in a very readable format explains the theory and how it affects us in daily life. With my normal short attention span, however, all I really heard him say was, "Yes, WOW is a credible philosophy," before I shifted my thoughts back to the respective merits of man-to-man versus zone defense.

I have been asked many times about the "Barnyard" nickname, and I honestly cannot remember its origin. To the best of my knowledge, it came from my early basketball days, when I averaged 37.2 points per game (or maybe it was 7.2). My given name is Byron, which my mother still uses, but the rest of my friends and acquaintances call me Barnyard or Barney. I include this note here because you will be getting to know me in this book, at least in the context of Adams Golf. Since you might want to stop and say, "Barnyard, that was a bit questionable," you might as well have my correct name.

Why, then, should you consider coughing up your hard-earned cash to purchase this book? I can think of three reasons: 1) you're looking to pick up an idea or two that would apply to a start-up or entrepreneurial environment; 2) you've got some curiosity about golf and the equipment side of the industry; or 3) you're looking for a true "rags to some degree of success" story with no punches pulled in the telling.

In reading this book you will be sure to notice that I am not brilliant or unusually insightful. I have decent intelligence and, when it comes to the golf industry, an abundance of passion. If you choose to read this as a business-type book, then you'll see where I screwed up and where I made some good calls, and I'll be as forthcoming as I can remember. I want to be clear on one thing, you'll read about how I (not we) made mistakes. Maybe I didn't always make the specific mistake myself (there's no question I made several), but I was the leader and that's the way it works. The person at the top gets to accept responsibility.

First and foremost this is the story of how one obsessed person started from nothing and built a successful company. A significant learning experience led to a product introduction that had a lasting effect on the golf industry, and you'll learn how that happened. But the Adams Golf story is not about a series of brilliant decisions; no company is, not when the story is true.

I am no longer active in the day-to-day operations of Adams Golf; this was a decision that I'll dissect in detail, for it's not an uncommon situation in entrepreneurial companies. Happily, the WOW factor still exists. As the story unfolds, I'll detail the thought process of identifying certain key decisions, good and bad, that I made as the company grew. It's been oft written that mistakes are the best platform for learning, and you'll see that I own a PhD in that discipline. I'm just waiting for the diploma to arrive.

I had great plans to take a minimal writing approach with this book, but you'll see it didn't quite work out that way. As I shuffled through my memories I'd start writing about one thing and find that it was connected to something in the past, which I felt it was necessary to include for clarity. This is not a beginning-to-end, linear business story. Instead, it's about the beginning, survival, and the incredible early years, and ends with a very young company continuing to establish a market position in a difficult industry.

I cannot go forward without relating an anecdote, which in a way reminds me of the path Adams followed. Long (very, very long) ago in school we were given a test matching ten items in column A to ten items in column B. We were asked to draw lines connecting the two. I got them all right and earned an F for my effort. You see, instead of drawing nice, straight lines I connected each item from the two columns with a series of lines that looped, zigged, zagged, and required a great deal of effort to follow.

My teacher did not think it necessary to put forth the extra effort and obviously was unaware that she could have nurtured the beginning of a great humorist. Instead, I got to stand in front of the class—my own particular brand of show and tell. Yes, there was a laugh. Somehow it wasn't what I had in mind, as the class took great pleasure in my embarrassment. Because this was second grade, it must have been significantly traumatic, since I still remember the incident. Either that, or I'm entering the stage of life where the ancient past is much clearer than the recent past, so I can't seem to remember what I ate yesterday. Despite my teacher's efforts, I still see the occasional need to connect the dots in a series of loops and swirls. I figure anyone can do it with straight lines.

PART ONE

THE STORY OF ADAMS GOLF

ONE

DISCOVERING THE INNER ENTREPRENEUR

I didn't want this book to be the Barney Adams life story, but instead the Adams Golf life story. In order to accurately portray the latter, however, the former requires a brief illumination. I am a product of the 1950s, and was fortunate to receive some financial assistance for attending college. In those days my alma mater, Clarkson University, was known as Clarkson College of Technology. It was primarily an engineering school noted for a high degree of academic excellence. One might surmise that the chance to become an engineer with a degree from a fine school would have influenced my decision to attend this school, but in truth it didn't.

With zero money and no access to any significant funding, my selection of Clarkson was simply a case of least-cost analysis. I'd go where the financial aid made it affordable. For me, going to college wasn't about some esoteric wish for education. It was about seeking the best vehicle toward getting a better job, something I had in common with many from my generation.

The financial aid came with assorted jobs and added to work I found locally. I managed to play sports, attend school, and graduate more with a sigh of relief than with any type of honors. Summers and holidays simply meant a chance for some gainful employment.

In 1956 I was fortunate enough to receive a scholarship from Crouse Hinds Company in Syracuse, New York, where my father worked. Crouse Hinds's offices were located twenty miles from Marcellus, a small town of about 750, where we lived. The scholarship was nice, but what really excited me was that it came with a summer job.

This job meant no more hiring myself out to dairy farms, spending the summers behind a hay baler or shoveling fresh manure from cows vigilantly checking to see if I was within kicking range. It was a real job paying $0.85 an hour, big-time pocket money in those days. The only downside was that I had to work in a factory—actually a black sand iron foundry seemingly designed and choreographed by Dante. But I was seventeen and very smart; after all, I had a scholarship. I figured the reason people worked there full time was that they were unlucky at birth and just not equipped with the mental faculties to handle greater challenges.

I resolved to be one of the guys, and not to show my intellectual advantage. Immediately, however, I learned a lesson that has driven me for the rest of my life more than any other one thing. As it turned out, a significant number of my fellow employees were smarter than I'll ever be. Not just street smart; I mean intellectually. I can still remember one guy who liked to spend his breaks reading books in French or German, two of the several languages he spoke and read fluently.

These men chose to work in that bleak environment for a variety of reasons. Some had to drop out of school to support aging or sick parents, or a young wife and child. Some had a fondness for the shot and beer offered by the corner saloon. Some had a lack of ambition. There were a million reasons why men ended up there, but it wasn't necessarily a lack of mental ability. My naïve little world started with a jolt.

In fact, it was much more than a jolt. It was like getting hit in the face by virtual lightning when I realized that I, too, could end up here with the flames from the furnace, breathing in the thick, black smoke that filled the air. I knew in that moment that unless I decided otherwise, this would be my life. The choice was mine. I had no family business waiting or fortune to inherit. If I'd gotten a little, shall we say, "casual" with my girlfriend, this was the place where I'd have to work to support my new family. It was as if, standing in that smoke-filled factory, there was a light shining on me. I was given a glimpse of what could be my future and the chilling knowledge that at seventeen I was at a crossroads. Quite honestly, it scared me, and motivated me. And to this day I still live with the fear that if I don't give my all, failure is just a step away.

As I relive that memory, it is as real now as it was then, virtually palpable, and I've seen the theme repeated at many different levels throughout my life. Think the corporate executive suites are filled with superior intellects, and the support workers are a capability notch down? To quote the rental car ad, "not exactly."

Over the years I have read many books on small business entrepreneurialism. To be sure I wasn't missing any new revelations, I returned to my favorite bookstore when getting ready to write this book. I perused the self-help and small-business sections looking for ideas and approaches to glean. In my own research and speaking to others I've learned that there is no one book that can serve as a guide for entrepreneurs. But the more you read, the more you pick up a paragraph here, an idea there.

I will admit to an idiosyncrasy—I love bookstores. They fascinate me. The knowledge of the world resides therein, and besides, you can buy mystery stories there. And one of the books I came across that day was *Jack*, the bestselling memoir of Jack Welch, CEO of General Electric. For many years I'd always harbored a long range envy of Jack. Who in business wouldn't? He's been called America's greatest CEO. He's loved by Wall Street. He sports a three handicap (for any non-golfer readers, that's in the upper 0.1 percent of those who play). He's a former champion at his club. He's phenomenally rich. He belongs to Augusta. What's not to envy? As I was reading his memoir a nagging feeling persisted, and then I remembered that he and I could have been working side by side. I, too, could have been loved by Wall Street. GE would have performed even better. And then, as my memory improved, the phrase returned: "Not exactly." The story takes a bit of telling.

My first job out of college was with Corning Glass (1962 to 1969), and in the style of the day I was transferred among branch plants ostensibly on my way up the proverbial management ladder. In those days "IBM" meant, "I've been moved" among us members of the working class. You went to work for a company, accepted their challenges, and understood that the inconveniences of moving were ultimately in your best interest. Now, looking back, I'm struck by the realization that my personal moves, while thinly veiled as promotions, actually had a different intent. I was systematically being removed from the corporate mainstream. If Corning could have opened a facility on the moon, I would have been issued a space suit immediately. Today, accompanied by a little wisdom from age, I can understand why.

I was a lousy corporate employee. Not incompetent, just lousy. Yes, I did my job and performed well, but doing my job was a diversion from my real goal in life, which was to run the entire corporation. Somehow I felt I had been given the gift of great leadership and could never understand why, with this gift, I hadn't ascended to my preordained position. It certainly was not a case of poor communication. I often provided top management with plans, objectives, and strategies, all designed to move the company forward and me upward.

In late 1969 I found myself in Shawnee, Oklahoma, in one of those "do well here and the next step is big time" moves. Shawnee was physically and maybe culturally one of the most distant branch plant postings, but I liked the area and the folks who lived there. I still do.

The product line, a ceramic-based, fire-retardant roofing shingle, was struggling. It was brittle, and tended to break under the weight of roofers. Essentially, Corning had built a facility to manufacture a product line that should still have been in development. Within months of my arrival, Corning decided to do more R&D and moved the technology into a fully-staffed facility in Kentucky, which meant all of us in Shawnee were out of work. As I look back now with better understanding of the corporate decision-making process, it occurs to me that someone had decided to move the facility before my "promotion." The time gap was attributable to logistical issues. Most of the salaried employees in Shawnee were transferred to other plants, but wise heads understood this was a perfect time to gracefully remove a problem: Me.

They were quite nice and exposed me to several job offerings they knew I wouldn't take, and I found myself unemployed with eight weeks' severance pay (normally it would have been four, but they told me they felt so bad and loved me so much, they doubled it). A new chapter in my life unfolded before me. I was married with three children; I had no savings, modest skills (I'd spent most of my career as a field engineer and quality manager), and only the want ads for new career prospects. Spending years in one company in a series of manufacturing-related positions does not build up the proverbial network, and this was well before the outsourced staffing systems used today. I only worked in Oklahoma a few months and never moved my family from Pennsylvania, my previous posting with Corning. After my official separation, handled by the corporate office in Corning, New York, I returned to Pennsylvania, bought a newspaper, and turned to the employment ads.

Opening to the want ads, I came across an opening for a quality manager at a local GE facility, certainly something within my purview. So I answered. I made it to the interview stage and was informed that as part of the process they were sending me to Manhattan to interview with a psychologist. Upon learning this, I immediately decided that it would be one of the first things I'd eliminate when I took over GE. But for the time being I figured I should go for the job first. So I was off to New York. I didn't know what to expect, and what I found was a second-story office smelling badly of newsprint and cheap pipe tobacco. Its inhabitant, a man of indeterminate age behind a bushy beard, smelled worse than the office. Suffice it to say that he observed my negative reaction and quickly dispatched me to a nearby table, where I was given the first half of a two-part test.

The entire first half of the test consisted of a single essay question. It asked, roughly, "If you knew the end of the world was five days away, and you had absolute information, what would you do with your time?" I figured that since they knew I was married, the question was really aimed at finding out how well I was grounded. Five days represented precious time to spend with those I loved the most. So I invented a fellow employee, who I called Jackie, and on a scale of one to ten I thoroughly described her as an eleven. In my essay, which took the form of a story, I somehow convinced Jackie of the impending disaster and persuaded her to overlook the ocean with me. Of course, that wasn't all we did, and I carefully omitted no detail. On top of that, I didn't include a single a word about my family, peace of mind, the greater good, or ice cream. Just Jackie and me.

To this day I have no idea what brain synapse brought on this response. One might say immaturity, and I'd have no defense but to say I think it was something more. Somehow, though I really needed a job, the entrepreneur in me was screaming out: "You are an individual, not a classification!" Whatever I was, I wasn't the model of a good corporate citizen.

The second half of the exam consisted of true-or-false and multiple-choice questions, which I attempted to answer as if I were one of the psychopaths found in my mystery books. Later, when I returned to GE, I spoke to the man who would have been my boss had I been hired. I confessed that I couldn't handle the process, and told him what I had done on the test. He cracked up, and told me he agreed with my analysis of that part of their system, but added that GE truly was a great place to work and that he would go to bat to get me the job. He was successful. I received an offer, and even though I had a family to feed and only five weeks more severance coming, I turned it down flat.

I'm sure had I accepted the job it would have only been a matter of time before Jack Welch plucked me out of the organization and installed me in my rightful place in top management. I really liked the guy who would have been my boss, but in a moment of rational thought I knew that I didn't belong in a big company. I'd already proven that at Corning, which was a really good place to work, and accepting this job would take me out of the frying pan and back into the fire, where I didn't belong.

While it was nice that I was reacting to some kind of inner drive to be independent, that independence wouldn't give me much solace while waiting in line for an unemployment check. Returning to Oklahoma to pick up my things, I bought the local newspaper and as was my habit, turned to the employment ads. There, I saw advertised a position selling equipment to supermarkets, which I figured was perfect for me. I had no sales experience, no industry or product knowledge, and the ad said the territory would be Southern California. I had never even been west of Oklahoma. Still, I replied, they interviewed me, and for reasons I'll never fully understand, I got the job.

Despite my incompetence for the position, the interviewing process took no time, and the training even less. It was the business equivalent of a "letter to Garcia." I was given a territory (Southern California), samples, a price sheet, and a partial customer list, and was wished good luck.

I left for a section of the United States I'd never seen before. Upon my arrival at LAX I learned that part of the airport was restricted because a movie was being filmed. When I got on the bus to our motel, the driver announced that he was really a comedian making meal money between gigs, and proceeded to rehearse his routine over the bus speaker system. Here I was, just in from Shawnee, Oklahoma. Talk about a message that things were going to change. All I had to do was figure out where to live, start earning enough to move my family, learn the business, and learn how to sell—not just my product but how to sell, period. You can attend forty-one seminars on entrepreneurship and never get a crash course like this. Oh yes—in the interview one thing had been "overlooked." I learned I was working on a draw against commission. In other words, I had about six months to produce or it would be back to the want ads.

When you make a sales call as a representative from Corning or GE, you are accorded a certain amount of respect. But make the same call as the janitor/sales VP of US Start Up, and after driving an hour through traffic you may find your contact has decided to take a long lunch, have a root canal, or reorganize his sock drawer. Whatever the plan, appointment or no, you weren't featured; in fact, you might have been erased. My supermarket job was only slightly better than being at US Start Up.

The company had neglected to tell me a few things in my non-training, most notably that that our number-one competitor was based in Southern California and they had about an 80 percent market share. Further, my predecessor had a bit of an alcohol problem; my potential customers hadn't seen anyone from our company for years and were frankly quite happy with the arrangement.

One of my early sales calls was a classic. The customer was the largest in my territory, the buyer infamous for being nasty to sales reps. Undaunted, I made an appointment and showed up the prescribed ten minutes early. Mr. Charm saw me waiting from his office some hundred feet away, and without standing up yelled to me to come over. When I got to his desk he said, at full volume, "Who the hell are you and why are you here?" I stammered out some kind of response, lapsing into my product pitch. Interrupting, he said (still at full volume), "Get the hell out of here. I have a vendor. Your stuff isn't any better and you're wasting my time." He wasn't kidding, and by this time the entire office was watching and enjoying the show. I made it back to the exit, which was a Herculean effort considering that I felt about two feet tall by the time I arrived.

I don't remember how I got to my car or where I was able to stop and relive the experience. I do remember thinking I could wait till the S.O.B. was heading for his car after work and accidentally brush up against him, but my corporate training kicked in. I decided to review the situation and see what I could learn. First, despite his nasty act, the buyer was right. He had capable vendors. I wasn't prepared to offer him anything he couldn't get from them, so I was, effectively, wasting his time. Further, this condition wasn't his alone. It would be the case with every call, so if I were going to be successful I had to become more than a body in the waiting room. He did me a favor that day, and later became my biggest account as the territory developed. But the lessons learned were invaluable, and completely different from any formal training I had received. This book isn't about my supermarket selling experience, however. It's about how I survived at Adams Golf facing odds that seemed impossible. A bit of insight gained from my early experiences made that survival possible.

TWO

IT ALL STARTS

"Well, Barney," people ask me all the time, "How did you get into the golf business?"

It's a tough question to answer. I don't want to be rude and offer a halfhearted reply, because to tell the story takes much longer than one would expect.

The real question is, how did someone like me, who didn't grow up working in the industry, get involved? Over the years I've observed three basic avenues: 1) You hire on in a beginning (or advanced) position and good performance moves you up to a top spot; 2) Your company acquires a golf manufacturing operation, and having performed well in other divisions you get a chance in a market dear to your heart; or 3) You sell your business and now have the opportunity and financial strength to start or invest in the golf industry, your lifelong passion. My path didn't take me down any of those avenues, though.

Instead, I had a long and distant affair with golf equipment. I wasn't one of those "handy" types with a workshop in the garage and everything neatly in place. Quite the contrary, in fact, as anything I tried "hands-on" was destined to total failure. As cluttered as I was on the exterior, my mind required that I understand how and why things worked. Not cars, radios, or computers, per se, but golf clubs.

It started with my caddying days at the Onondaga Country Club in Syracuse circa 1952, when I first watched the love affair between golfers and their equipment. Later, while at Clarkson, I learned that my future most likely lay in business. I started out in engineering but learned early on that I was out of my league. After six years I finally graduated from the business school, then had a couple of job offers including the one from Corning, where I worked as an applications and quality engineer for some years. I bring this up not as an attempt to establish my technical capability, but because my engineering background is essential to a thought process that I use to this day. Because of this part of my history, some folks have referred to me as an engineer. And yes, that was my title for a couple of jobs, but I have too much respect for the engineering degree, which I did not earn, to lay false claim to one.

Corning put me to work in their television division, which supplied most of the glass envelopes in television sets during that era. Because glass is too fragile to stand up to continual inspection, we sold it on a performance basis. This meant that when a customer had a production problem, my job was to investigate and determine where the problem had originated. The process involved careful investigation of cause and effect, often including statistical analysis, and I spent four days a week in customer manufacturing facilities performing variations of that function. Years later in my range days, while custom-fitting, I used essentially the same approach. For all practical purposes I was still an applications engineer working on the complexity of variations in the golf swing and equipment, trading the manufacturing environment for the driving range.

During my early years at Corning I sent my resume to the leading golf equipment companies of the time. I don't think they worked together, but the responses I received from each were almost identical: *No*, as in no experience, no job. The rejection was a disappointment, but it never dulled my interest in the business. I also played golf, but equipment became a constant source of study.

I'd ask myself why one stiff-shafted driver would feel wonderful and another feel awful. This was back in the days of steel shafts and persimmon heads. I carried these and other thoughts with me over the years while hitting nine million practice balls in order to become a decent club player, carrying a single digit handicap at the course where I regularly played. And while that is pretty good on balance, when you watch Bolt, Hogan, Nicklaus, Palmer, Snead—the stars of that era—you know what good *really* is.

Certainly my golf game is not worthy of mention for its skill level. But with years of practice, zillions of range balls hit, personal experiences with equipment variations, and endless curiosity, I managed to store thousands of hours of data in my mental computer.

One day in the early '70s a friend told me of a guy I had to meet, Dave Pelz, whom he described to be as nutty as I was. I didn't think we were nuts. In fact, after we met, I thought he was just serious about equipment, and that *we* were the normal ones. I first met Dave in Maryland, and made a modest investment in his company, which manufactured putters and putting teaching aids. I went to my first PGA Merchandise Show with him in 1973 at The Disney Hotel. Major companies were centrally located in the lobby, while small companies like Dave's were in motel rooms on the outskirts. I really don't remember much other than that it was *the* PGA Show and that I was there.

During this period I lived in Dallas, where I managed a small company that made steel shelving used primarily in supermarkets. I spent nearly ten years working in the supermarket industry, all on the equipment supply side. I recommend the experience to anyone as, at the very least, an education in job performance. The average chain store in those days worked on 0.8 percent profit margin. We had cost discussions that started in pennies and went to fractions.

Over the years I stayed in touch with Dave, made the annual trek to the PGA show, and along the way became friends with Tom Crow in his very early days as founder of Cobra Golf. I can remember taking Tom's Bafflers (railed persimmon fairway woods) around with me, showing them to anyone who would listen. I stayed in the supply side of the supermarket industry during these years, eventually ending up in Silicon Valley, at a company that made microprocessors programmed to reduce energy usage at the store level. Divorced and with three kids in college, it was imperative that I continue gainful employment but, once again, I moved. This time I went to work for a venture capital group focused on the semiconductor industry, where I was used in smaller companies to add my expertise to their start-up staffs.

I bring all this up because of the pattern. I didn't realize it consciously at the time, but it was all about going out on my own. Working as a hired gun provided great challenges and good money, but no real affinity for the products at hand. I was single, living in the San Francisco Bay area, had access to a fine golf course—all in all, not bad duty. These were all very good qualifications for an entrepreneurial venture and, sure enough, in 1982 the phone rang.

It was Dave Pelz, calling from Abilene, Texas, where he had moved from his native Maryland. He had found financial backers for his revolutionary new golf clubs, called Featherlites. "Barney," he said, "Come to Abilene. I need you to run my company. We have the greatest new idea in golf." I had heard of his product. In fact, *Golf Digest* had run a cover story on these super-light clubs that were going to transform the game into a source of joy and happiness for the average player.

Being the highly experienced executive that I was, I didn't jump into the decision over the phone. Instead, I went to Abilene, spent an hour looking at the facility, and then agreed. Some might think leaving the Bay Area for Abilene a bit questionable, requiring analysis of my due diligence. I think we played golf during the visit. I may have looked at some numbers, but I seriously doubt it. You could have renamed me Captain, because my ship had just arrived. This was the golf business, folks. My dream was coming true.

I don't know if my progression into full-time employment in the golf industry is of any value from a business perspective. Reading it for accuracy, I don't see anything that is out of line. It's almost as if I was destined to end up where I did, and maybe that's worthwhile advice—to follow your heart.

Yet as I write this, caution bells are sounding. If you have a passion and you are able to make it your life's work, can it turn on you? Market forces, borderline decisions, things you can't control all can work against your pure effort to succeed. There's also a chance that, like some, you'll lose your passion. And for most of us, our passions are so few and far between that losing them is simply not something we can afford. I've talked to doctors who loved medicine, who trained their whole young lives to enter the profession. But by the time we had our conversation, they wanted out.

Every year at the PGA Merchandise Show, people would come to the Adams Golf booth asking for a name so they could leave a résumé. This might seem normal for a trade show. One of the functions of a show is to connect people in the same industry. Except in this case, several of the résumés were from people outside the industry. The PGA show is supposed to be for golf professionals, retail buyers, and distributors. But it didn't take a genius for an outsider to wrangle a pass, and every year the same thing happened. The résumés themselves were interesting. Doctors, lawyers, CEOs,

PhDs—it was an amazing collection of highly talented people from other industries who all shared a passion for golf.

One time at the show I was talking to one of our newer staff members, and he asked how we handled résumés, as he'd just been approached. I told him it wasn't unusual, and we had designated someone to collect them. The review process would commence after the show when we were home.

I went on to tell him about the quality of some of the people applying, and he'd looked at me with an incredulous expression. As if on cue, I heard a voice say, "Are you Barney Adams?" When I confirmed, he handed me an envelope saying he hoped I'd review the contents. After he left I immediately opened the envelope (it could have been a summons) and there was a résumé from a PhD in law who was tired of the profession and wanted to follow his passion, golf. Suffice it to say that our employee just smiled and delivered the résumé to the growing stack. Another year I asked Ely Callaway if his company had a similar experience at the show. "Barney," he said, "We get hundreds."

I can't tell you that if you follow your passion you'll definitely be rewarded for it. All I can say is, do your homework and be as realistic as you can. At the same time, remember one thing: Do too much analysis and you'll never take a shot.

Sometimes you just have to go for it.

THREE

REVERSING NEGATIVE TRENDS

*W*hen I first arrived at Pelz Golf as a full-time employee, I encountered situations that weren't taught at any of the finer business schools or their lesser counterparts. This resulted in an awareness of what the corporate world likes to refer to as "a series of challenges."

The first was what I'll call negative sales. This was not the same thing as a classic downturn in the sales curve, but was a little more extreme—the UPS truck would arrive full of customer returns and leave empty. It seems a few problems developed that the numbers I had seen (or neglected during my failure to do due diligence) didn't reflect. Yes, Featherlites were a big story; they had been the hottest things in golf the previous season. Tour players used them and praised the results, for a while. Then they stopped. It turned out they had problems controlling the super-light clubs for anything less than full shots, and worse, shots under tournament pressure.

The golf industry is driven by innovation, and when the front pages of its major publications talk about being able to "buy a game," the demand is overwhelming, especially when the tour embraces the product. Pelz Golf wasn't the only company with ultra light clubs but it was certainly the leader. The equipment manufacturing industry as a whole did not embrace the Featherlite concept, though, and one painful lesson became evident. If the players on the PGA Tour use your product, that is a good thing. It's a hundredfold more powerful if your product is innovative. The market demand makes you look very smart, and people seek out your advice.

If those same tour players decide that they were wrong, that the product had serious flaws, it's a bad thing. The ensuing negative publicity is at least as significant, if not more so. Those other manufacturers who didn't embrace the concept remind everyone they were right and you were wrong. Not just now, but forever. Customers stop ordering and find reasons to send back what they have. No one wants to talk to you and you suddenly go from smart to dumb.

In the previous year, our shipments had been made to stores and pro shops across the United States. Some manufacturing problems had caused late arrival, often after the buying season. Had demand stayed the same, this issue could have been worked out. But since it had disappeared, the only issue for our customers was how quickly they could return the product and clear space for clubs they wanted.

When I first visited Pelz Golf, all the numbers I saw were shipments, and they looked good. But when the tour pros stopped playing Featherlites, the concept turned to poison. Competitors who had avoided the Featherlite craze fueled the bad news, and unopened boxes returned at a rate that burdened our ability to store them. This was my first experience (and not my last) with negative sales, and it was not pleasant.

There's more. On my second or third day in the factory I noticed a barrel of broken shafts. Upon inspection, I found that they were all broken in the grip, a flaw I had never seen before. Naturally I asked the manufacturing manager about it, and the answer I received was something like "Oh, yeah, we have a little problem." Only it wasn't so little. Stuffed away in a desk drawer were letters from attorneys relating to cuts in clients' hands from shafts breaking in the grip. I subsequently learned that the ultra-light steel shafts used in Featherlites had a design flaw that caused breakage in the grip area. In fact, one major shaft company had declined to make the clubs for that very reason. Some of the letters requested an apology, some an explanation and replacement clubs. Some were about having the company turned over to them upon completion of the legal process.

Our backers were some of the nicest people you could hope to meet. They had been very successful in the oil business, which had been thriving in Texas in the 1970s. But this was the early '80s. Oil prices plummeted, and with them the infrastructure of much of West Texas. We also had a little thing going called the savings and loan crisis, and guess whose bank was one of the first to cave in, calling in all of its loans? These were the "biggies," and many more surprises surfaced during my tenure at Pelz. It was a period with enough strife to send a normal person back to the safety of another business—any other business.

That thought never crossed my mind at the time, though. It probably should have, but it never happened. Between negative sales, legal threats, no money, and no source thereof, it was like *Survivor* twenty years before the TV show. In retrospect, the fact that I considered all those issues as daily problems defined the passion I brought to my job. I had always been very competitive in business but, until I entered the golf world, it wasn't a deep love for the products or the industry that drove me. Instead, it was the desire to succeed. Now, at Pelz Golf, all the business challenges were added to an abnormal passion for the products and the industry itself.

There is also another factor applicable to my situation: No one lied to me. It's entirely possible I turned a blind eye during my initial visit, or maybe I wasn't smart enough to understand what was really going on. It makes no difference. Once I signed on, people were depending on me to do the job. Sticking a toe in the water and running because it's too cold just isn't the way one accepts responsibility.

I checked the financial situation and determined we had a few months, perhaps more if I cut back expenses. Collecting the previous year's receivables (many now nearly a year old) would fund us for a while. Of course, when I initiated the collection process there were a few glitches. "What do you mean, 'in arrears'?" I'd hear. "I never got the product in the first place." Still, we stumbled through.

I knew that to survive we had to reduce the cost of running the business down to the lowest possible level and also figure out a way to turn our product into cash.

Cutting expenses meant cutting people, and that has always been one of my biggest weaknesses. A few months into my tenure, I had put the employment decision off too long, when I got a little help. It was standard in those days for me to work during the day, eat an evening meal, and then return to the office. If you worked late you missed dinner, as most of the Abilene restaurants closed early. And one night, while driving the five miles from my cafeteria back to Pelz Golf, I saw a glow on the horizon. At first I thought it was a fire. Then I thought *we* were on fire. But it was neither. Our building had every possible light burning and every door open, including the big shipping doors. But there was nobody there. Nobody. Frankly, I was nonplussed. After eliminating the possibility of alien abduction I was forced to conclude that our employees had just left the facility that way, including those in management, who apparently had no sense of ownership about the place. I had already encountered the "open facility" policy: friends and relatives were welcome to stop over, have a coffee, and chat—and this had been on the production floor. After all, it was golf, and golfers are interested. And when I stopped the practice, citing insurance issues, it was as if I'd insulted them.

The incident was a wake-up call, and I went through the painful process of paring down. A lot of companies, such as Corning, like to build branch plants in small towns where they receive financial considerations and are a major factor in the local economy. This is fine when things are good but, when the layoffs come, everyone shops at the same local stores, eats at the same restaurants, and guess who gets the malevolent stares?

When I say that cutting people is a personal weakness, I mean I've never gone through the paring-down process without gut-wrenching anxiety that lasted for days. Small companies are different. In most cases you hired the person, worked beside them, and were a part of a team. Even if you take over a struggling operation and everyone knows cuts are coming, it is still a very unpleasant task. But you cannot let your personal feelings get in the way of making sound business decisions. When you don't take appropriate actions regarding personnel, you hurt three groups: your investors, yourself, and the good employees who do their unfair share.

The world of small companies has a different set of personnel rules than those of the big companies. Starting up or taking over a smaller, troubled company is an incredibly difficult task. You cannot do the job alone; you have to surround yourself with the best talent you can find and work the hell out of them. I doubt if this philosophy shows up in any management books, but it is reality. In this environment you have to lead by example. You cannot expect extra effort from your employees if you are not personally leading the way. Your small company might not be able to compete with the big corporations from a salary and benefits perspective. What you have to offer potential employees is the chance to excel in their jobs without big-company politics and restrictions. Furthermore, there is the opportunity to be part of a team working toward asingle goal, the chance to win the game of business and enjoy a nice financial reward along the way. To some people, especially the kind you are looking for, that can be very attractive.

Those candidates who may be put off by your immediate salary limitations may not be the right fit for your company. But looking at the situation from a different perspective, it may be wise to consider taking a financial step back yourself, freeing up limited funds in order to hire key people who will greatly increase your company's chances of winning in the end. Did I do that? Absolutely. And sometimes, if the payroll needs overwhelmed available cash, guess who didn't get paid?

Even when you assemble the team you think will take your company to the goal you want, there will be roadblocks. Big corporations have the luxury of hiring talented people and, through training and experience, finding spots for them where they'll make the best contribution. But in a small company you have to hire the specific skills needed. This approach, however correct, has the potential for another problem. As I said, these talented people have experience and specific skill sets. Do they buy in to your goals for the business? Isn't it possible, if not likely, that their reaction could be contrary to your vision? These people aren't rookies, and they will have their own ways of doing things, their own concepts of how to win the game. It is extremely important that you clearly articulate your goals and request input so the goals are shared and belong to everyone. I cannot emphasize enough the need for clarity. Get all the cards on the table no matter how ugly the message. I must also be emphatic about one other point: Make sure you deal with facts, because it's easy to get caught up in emotion. Make sure that assembling the facts is an integral part of your process. You all have to be on the same bus headed to the same destination for the business to succeed.

What happens when someone doesn't work out? When you have to contemplate cutting one of your own team members, most likely someone you selected and worked beside? It's never an easy situation. I've been on both sides of the desk and know firsthand how the process can affect people's psyches, to say nothing of their financial and family situations, so I'll offer one piece of advice: When someone does get cut it shouldn't come as a surprise. You and your organization owe that person honest communication regarding his or her status, as well as offers to help him or her move in the right direction. Don't threaten, but treat the person honestly and fairly. It seems so simple and easy to do, but it rarely gets done well, especially in small companies where passion is the culture.

Inevitably, after you do make the decision, someone from your team will ask what took you so long. And there you have it. Your loyalty is to the people doing the job, to your investors, and, frankly, to yourself. It is just too difficult to burden the team with someone who does not share the established goals. Conversely, if you do not take action, you are sending a message that you don't really care, or that you care but you are not the leader who can win the game. This working arena has a fine line between success and failure; as the leader your message must be honest and consistent.

FOUR

WORKING THE SALES FUNCTION

*D*uring the process of trying to get costs and revenues at Pelz in order, I turned my attention to sales. One of our strengths was an association with one of the largest sales groups in the golf industry, E. J. Manley Company. They sold a line of soft goods under the Aureus brand and were preeminent in the industry. As in many industries, in golf the sales function is all about relationships. Customers in the golf industry then did not, as a rule, have professional buyers. At the on-course shop it was the golf professional who ordered product, and at the specialty retail store it was generally the store manager.

All companies in the golf equipment industry then, and to this day, relied heavily on their sales personnel. These field personnel learned who the good customers were, the folks who could move their product. They knew who paid bills on time, whom others watched as market leaders and, among competitors, that knowledge was universal. This meant that the good customers saw the best lines and the best reps, and even if your product was good you stood little chance of success without excellence in the field.

In the world of apparel, Aureus was at the top of the ladder. The brand was among the market leaders and had a strong field selling force. Pelz Golf was very fortunate to be part of their team.

Selling golf equipment properly was much more involved than making the initial sale. Making the sale was an opportunity to succeed or fail miserably. The main goal in selling to retail is not sell-in but sell-through, and therein lies the challenge. At the end of the day you depend on your customer's floor sales personnel to help move your product. This means that you need to educate them on the features and benefits of your clubs, motivate them to sell your brand as opposed to the ten others they carry, and make sure your product is displayed in a good position on the sales floor. Beyond that, your sales personnel should monitor floor sales results and revisit customers to keep inventories at proper levels.

Of course, marketing people were and are dedicated to campaigns that support the selling efforts, with the larger established brands having a distinct advantage in that area. This was a major issue for Pelz Golf, because we had to overcome what was perceived as the demise of Featherlite technology. The company's marketing strategy had come from its association with what appeared to be a breakthrough in club design. As for an actual marketing department, we had none, and faced with the negative public reaction to Featherlite, we had a significant task at hand. Fortunately, Dave Pelz himself had an excellent reputation as a product innovator, and the plan was to continue keeping costs at a minimum while we introduced a new line of clubs with his excellent design. If we could sell some new products and clean out the old stock, we stood a chance of surviving until better days arrived.

I had a basic understanding of the selling environment and agreed with the Pelz financial backers that the Aureus relationship was a significant asset. Aureus had over forty field sales professionals, years of experience, and considerable success. It was with great anticipation that I prepared for their annual sales meeting. It was my chance to present the new Pelz clubs and to set the stage for greater than ever success. Pelz didn't have a brochure or a sales manual at the time, so I worked nights preparing one. My plan was to overwhelm the Auerus people with the great potential of our relationship.

The Aureus sales meeting was very impressive. They had all the new styles of shirts, sweaters, and hats, as well as visuals on sales presentation, how to set goals, and how to optimize sales calls. The meeting lasted from 8:00 A.M. to 4:00 P.M. with a working lunch. As the time neared 3:45, I suspect the meeting's leader (the owner of Aureus) could feel my glare penetrating his back. The name Pelz Golf had not come up once, and after nearly eight hours I finally realized that our great sales team had little interest in anything but soft goods. Some of us just take a little longer to wake up and smell the coffee, and as I sat there it dawned on me that I was in left field. They were simply going about the business that mattered most to them.

I was less than happy, but in a fit of rational thinking I understood their position. Aureus management owned the shirt-making facility. Soft goods were their business, not clubs. And as I got to know the trade better I realized my plan never would have worked. Buying seasons for clubs and soft goods were different, and many of the reps were soft-goods specialists who barely played golf and certainly had no understanding or interest in that side of the business.

On paper the relationship looked great, but in reality it was a joke. And, to add insult to injury, the selling mismatch went even deeper. Whether due to late shipments or market conditions, customers had unsold Pelz merchandise in their inventory. Customers then told the Aureus reps to get the Pelz merchandise out of their shops, and that there would be no more buys from Aureus until they did. What did the reps do? Did they call Pelz Golf and ask for a return number, or try to work out a deal? Hardly. Instead, they told their customers that they'd pick the clubs up right away, as they were sure Pelz Golf would give them credit or just close the book, since the customers hadn't paid for the merchandise. When we later tried to collect on our shipments, we were told, "Your rep said..." and we were history. The new product line that was the basis for the company's growth was dead. We had no sales force to convince customers to work with us, and no marketing to overcome the Featherlite disaster. If there was any good news at all, it was that there was absolutely no question that we had to come up with a Plan B, and do so immediately.

Five-Minute Sales Seminar

I was an experienced salesperson by the time I got to Pelz Golf. In fact, I had been a damn good peddler, a term of respect I use to describe people who can go into the marketplace and survive.

So how and why did I fall asleep at the wheel? How did I fail? Looking back at the Pelz situation, the closest I can come to explaining my failure is to say that I was starstruck by my new title, Barney the President. Instead of thinking like a street rep, which is what I really was, I was attempting to look at the situation from a thousand feet away, obscured, shall we say, by my title. This disease, Title-itis, is not restricted to sales and it is insidious. It can strike in any area, and once it finds a willing host it will always be there, just waiting to erupt. The basic symptom is a failure to grasp the reality of a situation, as your vision is obscured by the ozone in your lofty position. This happens a lot in big companies. A sure sign is someone who surrounds himself with compliant yes men. Another symptom is taking credit for the work of people in your organization. A giveaway is the constant "My design, my company, my salesman, my toilet" spiel. Unless you are the sole employee of your company, I think the word you need to use is "our." I used to call on a buyer who was intensely disliked by his staff. They referred to him as "Good results are mine, bad ones are yours."

I have seen many cases of this disease. I've had it myself (twice that I recognize). You should be able to recognize it so that you can take preventative action. I've been told that autopsies on the Title-itis victims reveal an overabundance of omnipotence in their systems.

Sales is the one area where I see the most mistakes in small company start-ups. The selling environment for similar products is *not* the same, and it is not a level playing field.

For example, back in my days in Silicon Valley I was involved with a small company that manufactured a very good product. The inventor had correctly figured out a way to integrate his application into the larger manufacturing process of our potential customers. My role was to help the company get their sales moving, and I had hired a person from a large company with a similar product that wasn't nearly as good or as cost-effective as ours was. He had used his previous contacts to get an appointment with a potentially large customer, and I decided to go along with him to show the customer how serious our intent was.

Our call included a forty-five-minute drive through traffic, and we arrived on time. We then waited nearly an hour before the meeting commenced. To cut to the chase, the meeting went poorly. My guy was getting very frustrated, both by being kept waiting and by the client's apparent inability to recognize the value we offered. I found an excuse to leave, and our representative and I went for coffee.

The problem had nothing to do with our product. It was about human nature. Therein lies a major difference between the sales effort of a small company and that of a large corporation. Sure, our product was better, but look at it from the customer's perspective.

They knew nothing about us or our sales professional, even though in his big-company days he had successfully sold to them.

When you make a call representing US Corp, it's very different than representing US Start-Up. The former comes with years of established reputation, while the latter represents risk. If the client chose to integrate our product into their operation and had a minor failure six months down the line, it could be a disaster. Failure means downtime. People get upset. Fingers point. If the same failure occurred with US Corp, though, they would rush in and fix the problem. Life goes on, even if their response is the same as that of a small start-up. It's hard to point the finger at them. In their case, the problem is looked at as an aberration, while with a start-up it's the potential of a shoe ready to drop. Customers don't like to assume that risk, be it real or imagined. This lack of an equal playing field frustrated our sales professional to the point where he left us and went on to be very successful in a larger company. We both learned a lesson.

"Okay," you say. "I get the point. But how do I make the right decision? Sales is not my specialty. How do I find the right people?" Here is the honest answer: I don't know. And if I did I'd write another book, do seminars, and become very, very wealthy in a relatively short time. Further, I am skeptical of anyone who promises you the right answer. They may be able to provide some good tips, but nobody can guarantee success.

To set the stage for hiring a key person to manage the sales of "your baby," enlist as much outside help as you can afford. In my case, all I could afford was to ask around and try to read between the lines. A professional headhunter is a great asset, but you have to consider the reality of what you can afford. At the end of the day, with all the input you've gathered, you'll go with what feels right in your gut. And once you've made your decision, don't sit around and second-guess yourself. Instead, establish mutually acceptable goals and let the person do the job you hired him or her to do.

Selling in a start-up environment isn't about making calls; it's about strategy. In the case I described earlier, we ended up with a good business relationship but we didn't do so by selling the product. We convinced some of the customer's people to visit us, to see that we were a first-quality operation and that we had good, dedicated employees working for us. We sold ourselves before we sold our product. This is not the only approach to take, but it is a good example.

One final piece of advice is what not to do. I've occasionally met small business owners who have asked me for advice and analysis on their sales function. Generally, the CEO who contacted me did not have a sales background. Often, they moved members of their tech staff into field sales positions, especially with products of a technical nature. I'm a great believer in team-building from the inside, but sales is a profession and, accordingly, it requires professional skills. You cannot allow the face of your product, your company, to be a person who has good product knowledge but no background as a sales professional. Essentially, you are turning your company and your customers into the training ground. If the person shows real promise, then it's your job to see they learn the necessary skills through professional training.

FIVE

SAVED BY A NEW INNOVATION?

*T*en years from now, someone will be telling a story about a great putter that made a big splash in 2002, sold by Odyssey (Callaway). It featured two balls behind the putting surface as alignment aids and it was very popular, so much so that a later version featured three balls rather than two. When I say *very popular*, I'm talking about sales approaching the $100 million level. But unless the person telling the story is very old, he won't mention the father of the two-ball putter, the *original* three-ball.

In 1984 I told Dave Pelz we were in deep trouble. Our main line, Featherlite, was dead, and we desperately needed new product. As a club company we were associated with Featherlites. We'd lived by the sword and now it was sticking in our heart.

To complicate things, we couldn't come up with any new club designs. We had a one-man R&D department and, no matter how smart Dave was, he just couldn't produce new club technology every year. Still, Featherlites were our burden and it was going to take both time and a successful new product to win back the trust of the retail market.

Dave had a place called his "secrets room" where he could work on new ideas without interruption. It was not in the regular facility and I had never been there. After our conversation, we went there together and he showed me his ideas for two new putters. One had a small face with three simulated golf balls behind the hitting surface serving as alignment aids, and behind the three balls was a wing. The other had a wide face, which looked like a T shape, and also featured the three balls. Dave had reviewed both designs with an experienced patent attorney who was well versed in the rules of golf, as was Dave, and they agreed that both models were within the written rules on putter design.

Secure in his position, Dave had given one of the small-faced models to D. A. Weibring, a PGA Tour player he worked with on putting. D. A. liked the putter, and no wonder, because he made *everything*. Tour officials saw no problem with the design and, with D. A.'s success, the word got out. Golf magazines picked up the putter story. The unique look was highly visible and easy to under-stand, two things essential to introducing a new product. At the PGA Merchandise Show in Orlando that year, customers stood in line to place orders—some for the wide-faced model but most for the small-faced one. Dave had done it. His genius had saved the company.

I presided over our booth and set up multiple locations where we could take orders. I had known about the Featherlite phenom-enon at the PGA show, but had been an outsider. This time I was part of the company and was determined to use the success of the three-ball putter to re-establish Pelz Golf as a legitimate source of innovative equipment.

Dave himself was the main attraction, as he should have been. I tried to leverage his presence into orders from U.S. retail and pro shop accounts and set up arrangements with distributors outside of the United States. It's hard to put what was happening into perspective. Pelz Golf had hung its corporate hat on Featherlites. I was hired to oversee the distribution of golf's newest technology. By the time I got unpacked and learned about what was really going on, we were staging massive returns. Normally, for a small company, that meant death. But we were not only surviving, we were introducing a great new design, and customers seemed willing to forget about our past sins.

Near the end of that PGA show, a man came into our booth and introduced himself to me as a representative of the USGA (United States Golf Association) who, along with their European counterparts the R&A (Royal and Ancient), set and monitor the rules by which the game is played. I was aware of the association in a general sense, but had never had any direct contact with them. I did know one fact, though, which was that golfers play by the rules. It's perfectly legal to sell equipment that does not conform to the rules of golf, but virtually no one buys it and it is not allowed in any form of competition played under USGA rules.

The USGA representative asked me if we had gone through the standard procedure of submitting samples for approval before bringing the new putters to market. No, I'd never considered the procedure because I was unaware of its existence. Here I was, giddy with our show success and already planning to take advantage of growth opportunities. This question hit me like a ton of bricks. I knew we had consulted the patent attorney and that our experts felt the putters were fine, but the tone of the USGA representative's question was encased in a cloud. If I were afflicted with synesthesia the words would have been colored black. I knew this wasn't a good thing.

Everything Dave had done seemed logical to me, but I knew from a pure business sense that introducing a product without following normal industry procedure wasn't ideal. The future of the company was riding on successful sales, so this wasn't just one product to us—it was everything. Can you remember an instance from college days when you asked a professor a question and the tone of his answer indicated to you that he thought you were a moron? Well, *that's* what I remember feeling when I asked the USGA guy to explain the procedure to me. In his explanation he was clear that the association was aware of the product, and that "some members" of the equipment committee felt the putter violated their rules. I wasn't sure if the problem was the putter or their reaction to us not following procedure.

This was a crucial, painful decision for Pelz Golf in 1985. We had a hot product, millions in sales in the balance, and "experts" telling us the putter met the rules of golf. But "some members" of the USGA's equipment committee disagreed. I tried to be objective and ended up agreeing with Dave's position. Given some of the goofy-looking models of recent years, I think technically we *were* right. We decided to go ahead with the shipments. Later that summer, the USGA declared the small-faced model to be nonconforming, but the wide-faced model was fine. The relationship between the USGA, its rules, interpretations, and equipment companies is a long discussion unto itself. Suffice it to say that we came out on the short end of the final decision and it was devastating.

The market did not react to the split decision the way we had hoped. Instead, it drew the conclusion that all of the putters failed to meet the rules of golf. Putters came back in droves—small face, big face, it made no difference. The three-ball putter had become tainted with the word "nonconforming," and no one stopped to examine the difference between the small and large-faced models. The product was dead, and we didn't have the money or industry position to explain what had really happened. I can make all kinds of arguments about arbitrary decisions and our own diligence, but in the end, it was just another failure.

THE BANK SHUTS US DOWN

*W*e held on a while longer by starting the Pelz Short Game Schools, using our outdoor research facility. I figured with Dave's unique knowledge we could charge people in advance for a three-day school and it worked. The cash flow kept us alive as I desperately tried to find a buyer for the company, but there wasn't enough cash to pay operating expenses and the bank loans. I tried to convince the bank that we had a future as a short game school, but given our track record and the pressure on banks following the savings and loan crisis, it was a losing argument. I bought as much time as I could, but finally the bank had enough. They ordered us to shut down, liquidate, and use all revenue to pay back loans. I argued that our inventory was Featherlite golf clubs and three-ball putters, which no one wanted, but the bank didn't care. We were finished.

One night I was watching TV, searching for some kind of positive thought, watching everything and nothing at the same time. (Let's just say I have a serious case of "clickeritis.") I flashed through the equivalent of what is now the Home Shopping Network, and a thought occurred: They sell sporting goods. Why not golf clubs? The next day I called to schedule an appointment with the sporting-goods buyer at HSN. On the way to their head-quarters in Minneapolis I thought to myself, "Boy you've had some crazy ideas before, but this one might be a record-breaker." When I met the buyer, he explained that their formula for selling a branded product was to divide the retail price in half. Then they'd divide that figure in half again. If the retail price was $100, they would sell at $50 and buy at $25. If we could meet those parameters, they were interested.

Today there are dozens of cable outlets that not only sell product but that specialize in certain types. This was in the dark ages of the television sales approach, though, and this one company sold *everything*.

Their formula was good news to me, as my lowest selling price was higher than the formula dictated. We had assembled clubs and inventory that totaled thousands of sets. They gave me a nice order with the promise of more if the product sold well. They moved something like two thousand sets in the first three weeks! I was, frankly, astounded. I'd have bet the ranch that we would never sell our inventory, and here we were scrambling to keep up with their demand. Instead of thinking about the bank, I was thinking of the contribution this would make to the guys who backed Pelz Golf. In my book, you couldn't find better people than Tony Andress and Hal and Jack McLothlin, and I wanted to provide them with some good news for a change.

Even after this success, there was one last twist. The clubs sold so well that HSN not only took our entire inventory, they wanted more than we had. I contacted our source for club heads and found some unused inventory that we were able to buy cheaply. I added people to our assembly crew and proceeded with an increase in sales. Then the bank shut us down again! We had an agreement to spend X and produce Y, and when I exceeded costs by buying more heads and increasing labor, they weren't interested. I showed them the extra revenue they were getting, but my pleas fell on deaf ears. I argued that if they'd continue lending us the money, we could keep the company going and they'd come out *ahead*.

I think the banker I dealt with was a prototype for the USGA. He carefully explained to me that the bank had no interest in Pelz Golf and we should just finish the deal as agreed. Did we concede? Of course not. We just kept an extra set of hidden books for payroll and expenses, and when the bank received the extra revenue they chalked it up to efficiency. Ultimately we ran out of inventory and, at the order of the bank, we auctioned the remaining assets of Pelz Golf in 1987.

We had failed, or, more accurately, I had failed. And let me be clear that I know I failed. I was the CEO and the company cratered, so it was *my* failure. That's how the system works. I could provide documents explaining how the deck was stacked against me and how I had really performed brilliantly (I hadn't), but no one wants to hear that. I wanted to be the person in charge, and ultimately I had invested all of my modest life savings in Pelz Golf, so the finality of the ending was painful for me on several fronts. The lesson learned this time around was that the game rewards those who win. Trying alone doesn't reap any awards, so for my efforts I got none, deserved none, and that's the name of that tune.

What could I have done differently? Well, first I should have recognized immediately that Pelz Golf was in a street fight, and instead of repeating my title and waving around my copy of the Marquess of Queensberry rules I'd have kicked some ass. I would have listened to no one with a vested interest, and instead I'd have gone to our customers and listened carefully to everything they said. Especially the bad stuff.

I'd also have set up the most draconian of cash budgets and cut costs until Dave and I were personally doing assembly and cutting deals with suppliers. I can go on, but you get the idea. Hindsight is always 20/20. My failure was that I didn't spend time with our customers to learn firsthand what they wanted from us because I was too busy being president. If I had spent more time with our customers, I wouldn't have spent any time on the sales organization that turned out not to exist anyway. Instead I would have concentrated on coming up with something to sell, and if that meant shutting down for months it would have been the better path to take.

Still, out of that failure I learned about the incredible power of TV to sell product. Somehow that lodged in my brain, and was scheduled to resurface at a later date.

SEVEN

THE BEGINNING OF ADAMS GOLF

Pelz Golf was over, our inventory sold down to scrap. All that was left were some desks, tables, and a few fixtures, nothing with much value to the general public. It was a tough time for me personally. Dave had an opportunity to expand his short game schools and moved on. I was surrounded by my failure, broke and with no employment prospects at hand.

Any sort of rational analysis would have led to the conclusion that it was time to leave, find work of some kind, and chalk up my misadventure in the golf industry to experience. I can tell you that I've relived this thought process countless times and cannot begin to explain what was motivating me. The only answer must be that I was blinded by passion.

Despite everything that happened, I still went to work early and left late. I was still in the environment of making clubs, and I convinced myself that, although sidelined by some setbacks, it was an industry I loved and, if properly directed, I could identify a future for myself in it.

We were under bank orders to auction off any remaining assets, so I borrowed some money from my brother and a couple of friends and bought everything that remained at the auction. I then lucked into an assembly contract for my newly formed company, which I initially named B. H. Golf. Pelz had liquidated its inventory with the Home Shopping Network, and after I started up, HSN contacted me expressing interest in going forward with the program. Fortunately for me and my finances they were basically interested in a test to see if there was still consumer demand. I proposed to the bank that we had a business opportunity, which was ironic considering the way things had ended. The bank people were too polite to laugh me out of their office, but I got the message.

HSN sold enough to keep my small operation going for a year. My approach to the new start-up centered simply around minimal overhead, immediate payment, and generating sufficient cash which would be saved and provide funding as I planned for a future in the golf equipment industry.

This slow growth also gave me enough time to figure out a business plan, not so much in the formal sense, but in terms of deciding where to go next. It was 1987, and analyzing the golf industry I determined that there was a potential niche in the components area. This is the supplying of heads, shafts, and grips to the thousands of "do it yourself" club-makers who are hobbyists or small businesses. I planned to upgrade my service level by pre-measuring all components, thus insuring high-quality product upon final assembly.

Starting with our manufacturing contract, I moved into what turned out to be the fastest growing segment of the golf industry for years to come. Furthermore, it was a cash and credit card business; assuming any degree of decent components sales we'd be able to pay the rent and continue to build cash. My small staff in Abilene could handle the business with me visiting only periodically. So I decided to return to Silicon Valley and earn a steady paycheck. I knew it wasn't where I wanted to be long-term, but my start-up was fueled by passion, not a solid plan. By taking a job back in the Bay Area I was able to keep my salary out of B.H. Golf and even negotiated for some time to visit Abilene. The objective was to increase funding to the point where someday I could start a full-time golf equipment business.

The PGA Show was held every January in Orlando, Florida, where members of the golf equipment industry set up booths to display their products to potential customers—not consumers, but golf shop operators, retailers, and overseas distributors. The show, an industry centerpiece with a waiting list of businesses hoping to attend, lasted four days. It's difficult to adequately describe what the PGA show was like in those days. I wasn't the only guy in the industry fueled by passion, and some of the others had the money to present show booths spectacular in size and presentation.

The Pelz Golf assets I had bought included seniority at the show, so in January 1987 I rented a ten-by-ten booth and set up shop. I did not have a great location, but I learned to raise and lower my voice commensurate with the sounds of flushing toilets behind us. I drove the booth to Orlando, set it up myself, and watched longingly each day as customers walked by averting their eyes.

Not discouraged a bit, at the end of each ten-hour show day I walked across the street to the main hotel, the Peabody. I had attended many trade shows in my supermarket days and had been trained by experts on how to work a room. So I went to every cocktail party, not for the drinks (okay, it served as dinner), but to learn. Every industry has leaders in all phases. Many are not evident, and I wanted to identify who the influential customers were, what manufacturers were the most respected, and what members of the press got everyone's ear. I spoke to sales reps to learn what they did, and I assumed nothing and tried to sponge up everything I could. Some of this information I retained from my Pelz experience, but this time I had no name, no product, and no brand awareness. I was starting from a much lower level.

The parties effectively turned the show into a fifteen-hour day—longer when you included the drive to my motel, which wasn't exactly the Ritz. Some people consider trade shows to be a vacation, a place to have a good time, to see and be seen. Not me. I had a series of objectives, and *vacation* wasn't on the list. Orders were written at the show, so I was told, but I was somehow missing that process at the time. I knew I was failing in that regard, but I felt I was paying my dues. I was at the show under my own name, which had zero industry impact, and I had to earn my position. I recollect long periods of solitude at my tiny booth in those days.

After the show I dismantled the booth, drove it back to Abilene, stored it in our building, and headed back to San Francisco. For the record, "our building" was the old Pelz facility, which we shared with an environmental testing company. "Shared" might not be the most apt description of the arrangement, though. They paid rent, so they got priority. We bartered, our rent fit my budget, and we existed. As time passed, I received good reports on component sales, our cash situation improved, and in Silicon Valley I got involved with a small company, Intertest, that made sophisticated testing equipment for semiconductors.

The big show for that industry was the Semicon West show held annually at the San Mateo County fairgrounds. The guys in Intertest were as excited about the Semicon show as I had been about the PGA show. Let me be clear about one thing here: My passion for the testing company was in doing my best to help it succeed, and to that end I gave it my all, but the products themselves invoked no such feelings. I went to the show and helped set up and work the booth. The show opened at 8:30 a.m., and after what seemed like forever I figured it was getting close to lunch. I glanced at my watch, only to learn that it was 9:00! A short half-hour in the booth had already felt like half a day. "Barney," the inner voice screamed, "You don't belong here!"

I discussed this tale of two trade shows with my friends and Jackie, the woman who would become my second wife, and it became obvious that they realized where I belonged well before I did. I couldn't just abandon the testing company, so I approached the venture capitalists who backed them with an idea. We were a small company lacking the resources to adequately finance our overhead, and our area of test equipment was limited. So why not find another operation with other forms of testing to the same customers and combine the two? The backers agreed. I got lucky finding a company that fit perfectly, and in a relatively short period a deal was made. The CEO of the other company wanted to stay on and I wanted to leave, so everyone was happy. I was owed some money and I negotiated to take it monthly over the course of three years, intending to go back to the golf business full-time using the cash on hand to grow the company and still not have to pay myself.

After the happy ending of my experience with the test company I packed my few belongings in my automobile and headed for Abilene, a long drive I'd made several times previously but this time with a sense of exhilaration that made it a breeze. I was on my way to *my* company in an industry I loved. I had some money and a plan, as if my entire working life had been in preparation for what awaited me.

EIGHT

THE MORNING OF THE
GREAT AWAKENING

My first job upon arrival in Abilene was to secure lodging, and I had that covered. The Ramada Inn was an old friend from previous visits. It provided an adequate room and was within walking distance to Luby's cafeteria. In fact, the room was more than adequate, as I had negotiated a monthly rate for a deluxe room, which meant it included a queen size bed, an easy chair and a remote control for the nineteen-inch TV.

The B. H. Golf corporate headquarters, a metal building, was only a few minutes away. Metal buildings, while quite functional, can be a bit noisy without significant insulation. In Texas we have angry weather. Things like soft rain and light breezes are the stuff of books written by Yankees. We get gully washers, winds that bend flagsticks in half, and that West Texas combination of a frog-strangler followed by a tornado. I never had to check the weather, as the various critters that co-inhabited our building tipped me off. A note here to the environmentalists: I can personally attest that constructing a metal building in a field does not displace the local critters. They just move in with you. Their degree of movement forecasted what was coming, and we were so in touch with the sounds that we not only recognized the movements, we knew who made them. "Must be a rainstorm coming. The mice are really nervous today," I'd say. Then, upon further observation, I'd see the armadillos moving and realize it was going to be more than that. "Probably a gully washer. We'd better get our desks away from the leak areas."

When you work in a corporation, your process is designed around efficiency, and generally the forces of Mother Nature are confined to upsetting the commute. We had no commuting problems, but weather had a different effect. "Sorry, I have to hang up," I'd say to a customer over the telephone. "It's hailing and I can't hear a thing." When I worked late I closely communed with various rustlings, screeches, and ever-present bumps in the night that were part of daily living in West Texas.

I'd previously experienced the weather phenomena in my time working for Dave, so no matter what the weather was that first day, I was in heaven. I enjoyed the sounds of the metal building, and for the first time in my life I was walking through the doors of my own company, not visiting, but to stay. I was now 100 percent on my own, in a business I loved, and if this description sounds euphoric, it's understated.

Any reasonable, experienced businessman would have arrived with a business plan, ideas about product and staffing, especially considering that I had built up an adequate starting cash position. But the only thing I had was the sense that financially I had bought myself some time. To say I was blinded by passion is not sufficient. As I write this and relive that first morning, the memories are very strong. I do not have the ability to describe the pure joy that I felt, but I remember it as I write. I knew the mortality rate in small business, and I knew that the first months, even the first year or two, were critical. But I also knew in my heart that I would succeed. It was going to work. I was as sure of that as breathing.

I arrived at dawn that first day and my first order of business was to set up my office. The remaining Pelz assets I had purchased from the bank consisted mostly of old furniture, a few tables, some heavy racks, and a few gauges for measuring golf equipment. There were lots of desks, huge wooden behemoths that were virtually unmovable. The "finance" desk didn't belong to anyone; it got its name because that's where we kept our books. Our system was strictly cigar box accounting. We kept track of cash and credit card sales and measured our success by having more in the box at the end of the day than when we started.

I settled into the finance desk that first morning about 6:30 A.M., Mr. Executive, all alone having a little financial review. After making coffee and sitting for a few minutes I started opening drawers (but in a very executive manner). Nothing was unusual; the green pad where we entered deposits and expenses was in the large middle drawer. It was this pad that gave me the daily status, and over the preceding months it had always been the information I asked about first when I called in from California.

The desk seemed in order until I opened the lower left-hand drawer and found it full of paper. I started to dump it out, thinking it was trash from some previous occupant, but then a couple of items caught my eye. Much to my astonishment there were a number of overdue collection letters from attorneys, and as I read more I learned that they were representing my suppliers and that the dates were current. I read through the entire stack of letters several times, first in denial then slowly with a recognition that spread across my consciousness like an onrushing disease.

To this day I can't quite describe the feeling. I became physically ill. I cursed, cried, broke a finger punching a wall. All the euphoria, all of my dreams came crashing down on my head and I hadn't even been in the office for thirty minutes. Those letters meant that I didn't have the nest egg I thought I had from my current and previous operations. Far from it—I was tens of thousands of dollars in the hole. My name and my business were a travesty.

Over the previous months when I had called in about our status, the reports had always been glowing. In retrospect this was clearly a manufactured response, especially as my arrival grew imminent. But as I sat there at the finance desk with my mouth agape, one thought was paramount: I was the dummy. My brilliant plan to finance a start-up was sophomoric and stupid. Well, maybe the plan wasn't that bad but the execution was pathetic. And to make things worse it was the same type of mistake I had made at Pelz. I was still operating as an executive so full of myself that I never considered the forces of human nature. In that regard I asked to be cheated, because I gave up control. The only way I could have made it any easier for someone wanting to use B.H. Golf money for personal expenditures would have been to send out a series of signed checks.

Was I unlucky? Sure. It didn't have to happen. But I spent the next several days in a deep depression. And while I never truly considered the act of suicide, I did calculate how much my meager life insurance would have yielded in the case of a fatal accident. At least some bills could have been paid.

NINE

HOW NOT TO FINANCE A BUSINESS

*E*ventually I started taking an inventory. How bad was it? Did I have any assets at all? Where I thought I had no debt and twelve months of working capital, I was actually on the collection list of every supplier I had. I wondered if the incident was an omen, a harbinger of future events. If you stop and think about it, the thought is logical. I'm starting up in a consumer product business with no technology and no real sales or marketing, just a desire. Now, to make matters worse, I had no money save my monthly check from the Silicon Valley deal, and that was supposed to serve as a small insurance provider. I don't think anyone would have blamed me if I had gone public with the story, admitted that the light had finally dawned, bankrupted the business, and gone about my way.

But that thought never crossed my mind. From whatever angle I looked at the situation, I felt I had no choice but to stay in the business. There were all these people I owed. It wasn't some company that owed them, it was me, so I did go public with the story. I contacted everyone I owed, and told them what had happened and that I would pay them back. Most were appreciative. When I called they told me they had been getting the runaround for some time, but they all wanted a schedule. My answer was the same to each. "You've been lied to all along and if I agree to a schedule it will be another lie. I'm going to pay you back. I don't know when and there's no sense trying to play hardball, because there's nothing here to get."

Somewhere during this process I was transferring the contents of my briefcase into my new desk (since I couldn't stand working at the one I'd originally selected) and I came across a checkbook. It was part of a personal credit line I had with a Silicon Valley bank from years past. I had used it a few times and always paid everything back, and there it sat, a $50,000 line of credit secured in my name.

Did I contact them, explain my current conditions, and ask if the line was still good? Nope. I just wrote a check for $28,200 payable to B. H. Golf, cleverly picking an odd amount to escape suspicion. When the check cleared I wrote two more, transferring all but a few hundred dollars of the full line.

Next, I used my cash available on the three credit cards I carried and built my stash. This was the beginning of a near Ponzi scheme I ran for several years. I don't remember how many credit cards I juggled, borrowing from one to make payments on another, yet somehow always managing to pay on time. It was well into the twenties, maybe thirties. I honestly don't want to remember. Ironically, my prompt payments identified me as a good credit risk and before long I didn't have to search out new cards. One day they just started arriving in the mail pre-approved.

It is ridiculous even to imply that my funding process had any merit applicable to the world of entrepreneurs. These were the acts of a truly desperate person. The fact that I was able to engineer this charade for years only underscores my overwhelming desire to stay in the business. And after I got over the shock, anger, and grief of my illustrious beginning, I had an uneasy respite from my financial morass and caught a break in a most unusual form.

Today, more than 90 percent of the heads used on golf clubs come from Asia. But back in 1988 it was more like 50 percent. I was an early pioneer in Asian sourcing. My main supplier was eager to continue dealing with me, agreeing to postpone payback as long as I paid for new shipments. Frankly, this surprised me. I could only assume he knew of my good character and solid reputation. Years later I found out that neither had any bearing. It was a government program designed to encourage Taiwanese manufacturing. Turns out if you made a product in Taiwan and shipped it out of the country you could submit your invoice to the Taiwanese government to get your money. Manufacturers could pay back at virtually no interest and had the crucial financing needed to build their companies. It was a good program in a country that didn't (at least then) have the variety of funding sources available in places like the United States.

Of course, the system depended on ultimately getting paid, and therein lay the problem my supplier faced. It seems he had made some questionable choices regarding his U.S. customers and was getting paid back very slowly, if at all. Since I started paying as I went, I actually helped contribute to his ability to stay in business while he struggled with his government. His unfortunate circumstance gave me time to source club heads, which was critical if I had any chance of going forward. Here we were, two entrepreneurs in two completely different countries with different cultures and regulations, yet the problems we faced on a daily basis were conceptually quite similar.

I could write much more about my battle to achieve credit equality, but the key point is that eventually everyone got paid. In some cases it took a long time. Some creditors received a negotiated amount and some received every penny owed, but I fulfilled my promise to each. It would be nice to be able to write that those people still remember, that they send me holiday cards, but of course I'm kidding. This was a major business predicament of my own making, and no one should congratulate me for paying a bill I owed no matter how extenuating the circumstances. Let me provide some baseline advice to all entrepreneurs. Do the job, succeed; no one wants to hear your sad stories. Just concentrate on winning the "game" of business.

TEN

YOU'VE GOT TO BE KIDDING ME

*R*emember my deal from the Silicon Valley, in which I negotiated a monthly salary over three years that would enable me to reinvest B.H. Golf's working capital to grow the business? Well, by now you know that the working capital turned out to be a working deficit, and that my Ponzi scheme had me paying interest on interest on interest. Technically my financial efforts passed no reality test but as I learned to live with them they seemed palatable. What follows, however, falls under the heading of "What doesn't kill you only makes you stronger."

About three months into my struggle to gain some momentum, one of the monthly Silicon Valley checks failed to arrive. I gave it a few days, figuring it must have been an error in the postal system, but when no check arrived in the subsequent days I decided to call. And while I can't quite say that what followed rates up there with the horrific first morning when I arrived at the opportunity of my dreams, trust me when I tell you that if you wrote it as fiction no one would believe it.

Apparently it had only taken a few weeks for the new management to develop an acrimonious relationship with the venture capital group that funded the merger, and they associated me with what they viewed as the bad guys. When I spoke to the CEO who had taken over the combined companies, he told me it was my fault they weren't getting along, and that I should look to the venture group to honor my salary because it sure wasn't coming from him. When I called my contact at the venture group who had helped negotiate everything, he told me he'd like to help but he was going into a major fundraising period and would be "out of pocket for a few months." He made it clear that this was my problem to work out with the operating company, and wished me good luck.

Ah, devastation and despair—my old friends. I couldn't believe this was happening. And much like that first day in Abilene, I went into shock. All these years later I can still remember vividly the anger, the utter frustration I felt in this moment I had endured the worst kind of financial chicanery, had no business plan, no product ideas, and no sales. Looking back, the misplacement of the B.H. Golf money had been an attack on my company and my dream. Exacerbated by the fact that it was my own fault, the effect was to make me physically ill. This time, the failure of the contract deal made me mad, as it was an attack on me. I had acted in good faith and the other participants had not. I considered it a betrayal of the highest order.

I did what any other rational person would do in this situation. I contacted a Silicon Valley lawyer, who said I had a solid case even though the amount involved was not a substantial figure. When I explained that I didn't have a dime and that his retainer would be a contingency I could sense a bit of waning enthusiasm on his part, but we went forward with the lawsuit anyway. The whole process took a couple of years (which did *not* help my financial crisis), and shortly after my litigation started the strangest thing happened. The new management team filed a suit against the venture group saying they had been promised financing that never came, and that those promises were the only reason they had agreed to the deal. Furthermore, they had a witness who would substantiate their claims—one Barney Adams. The venture group countered by claiming that the company failed to deliver performance as promised, and they also had a witness to these conversations—one Barney Adams. Incredible.

Let me get this straight. I'm suing for failure to support, by either or both groups, and they both want me as their key witness and the amount of their suit far exceeds my claim? If there was ever an opportunity to cut a deal this was it, as essentially everything depended on my testimony. It was also my chance to balance the books a little, and to get even with some of the garbage that had fallen on my head.

One other fact: my memory was pretty good back in those days. I knew exactly who had said what, and as much as I was disgusted with the venture company for ignoring my problem, my clear recollection was that they were right. Did I think of get-even scenarios? Did I try to come up with some "memories" I would be sure to benefit from? You bet I did. Who in my position wouldn't have? I could have "remembered" many promises that the venture group made and never delivered. With a little creativity I could have engineered a story showing that they (whichever side I picked) negatively impacted not only the new company but yours truly as well. But when it came time for the legal proceedings, it didn't happen that way.

When I was deposed, many of the questions I was asked were designed to lead my answers to the detriment of the venture group. I actually found myself in conflict with the company's lawyers. One would ask, "When X was promised in the meeting, did you feel it would be sufficient for the new group?" I would answer, "I specifically remember that meeting, and many others, because the theme was always the same: no guarantees. This was a performance deal. We'll get you started, but you have to perform."

The management's suit was dismissed based primarily on my testimony. I'd like to tell you that the venture group then asked for a private meeting with me, expressed their love and appreciation, and negotiated a happy ending. But what really happened was that my suit dragged on to a minor settlement roughly amounting to the cost of their continuing attorney's fees.

You might think this anecdote, while 100 percent true, was included as an example of my sterling character. If that was your thought, thank you, but it is not the case. As much as I was disgusted with both parties, my greater allegiance was to B.H. Golf. I knew I was in a fight for my business life and needed all my time and attention to even have a chance of succeeding. Getting cute with a lawsuit was out of my league. I clearly understood that, and the idea of staying focused is not a bad concept to embrace.

ELEVEN

OKAY, THIS TIME I'M REALLY STARTING

*W*riting this book has not only brought back memories, it's allowed me to look at situations from a historical perspective. It is now clear that the dual financial disasters that defined my beginnings in the golf industry were the greatest positive influences on my subsequent success. It's taken me years to understand this, but those experiences put me into a position of not being able to quit. I owed money, had no income, so any other upsets encountered along the way to my success were minor by comparison.

I was given the "opportunity" to start from so far in the hole that you couldn't calculate the odds of getting back to even. Moreover, the nature of my handicap was debt incurred in my name and in "my" industry. The challenge wasn't to succeed or fail, it was succeed or be disgraced. And it was time to start executing. Sure, my financing plan meant compound interest into the twentieth percentile, but you play the cards you're dealt...

Fortunately, the nature of the components business was cash and credit cards, so my first strategy was to increase sales. This involved calling hundreds of small operations, and I actively participated in the process. (Are you kidding? I was essentially the only staff that was left.) As I worked the phones, a flaw in my system became obvious. My customers loved the pre-measured product, but conversations went something like this: "Great, send me ten sets of Ping knockoffs."

I tried to explain that my service featured original designs and did not include knockoffs, but the customer's response proved that I had done inadequate research in setting up my components business. At that time much of the component industry growth was attributed to inexpensive imitations of successful brands, and failure to meet requests for these imitations meant limited sales. This was not an easy decision; given the start-up issues we faced my objective was to generate money. Lots of companies sold knockoffs and we could have developed a nice little business. I didn't fully understand it at the time but there was a lesson in front of me. I had started with hopes and ideals that included a set of standards. I could have deviated from those standards, but something wouldn't allow me to. Whether it was my passion or an inner sense of ethics, I just couldn't consider knockoffs. Seeing the handwriting on the wall, I sold my components inventory to one of my customers and turned my attention to assembled clubs.

I had read about a golf club company doing work with a process called nitrocarburizing. It was a finishing process developed by the automotive industry that was a rust protector and turned steel to a black color. Furthermore, it hardened the surface to a diamond-like degree. I had a vision of beautiful black, distinctive clubs that propelled golf balls great distances because of their super-hard faces. I was not the only company experimenting with this process, nor was I the only one working the concept of face hardness and performance. I developed a full set of nitrocarburized woods and irons. They were my original designs, and frankly, they were a good-looking product.

Of course, the clubs had a few problems. At the end of the day the hard faces did nothing to increase performance. It's one of those concepts that sounds good but doesn't stand up to analysis. We all want to hit the ball farther, and it seemed like a super-hard face could be a vehicle to more distance. Unfortunately it isn't; as long as the club face doesn't absorb energy, making it super-hard doesn't produce more efficiency. Unfortunately, the only true result of nitrocarburizing was that it was harder to make the clubs, but it didn't produce better golf shots.

There was also a second lesson to be learned. While I struggled with the face hardness issue, I saw ads in golf magazines by some equipment companies promoting the value of that very concept. I knew it didn't work, and while I recognized that the ads were carefully worded to avoid specific promises, the implication was obvious. My lesson was clear; I had to provide innovation, clubs that met their promise on the golf course.

Forget attempting to penetrate the marketing world with any story. I had no money, no staff. I also recognized another mistake of even greater magnitude. My initial product was a full set of woods and irons. They were a very good design, competitive with or superior to anything on the market, yet I was still making the same mistake I had made at Pelz, or at least a variation of it. I was good at looking at the bigger picture, seeing trends and needs, but I had this corporate mentality that caused me to underestimate the difficulties involved in getting the product to market. I had no business starting with a full set. It would have been much wiser to take any single club type, whether it be irons, wedges, fairway woods, or drivers, and apply the new technology, keep design and assembly costs down, and focus on just that segment of the market.

Because B. H. Golf was only me and not a team of experts, I had to think and act more specifically if I were going to have a chance to succeed.

It was also time for another big decision—to leave Abilene. I had married my companion, Jackie Caddell, and she had a job in Dallas some two hundred miles to the east. We didn't enjoy what you would call a two-person income, since mine was inconsistent at best, but we could afford a place to rent in Dallas and I made the drive many weekends. Despite all of my business struggles, Jackie never lost faith in me. Why, I don't know, because I was rarely the bearer of good news. She always just looked at the potential, and not because of a great lifestyle. I was usually exhausted on the weekends when I'd make the t drive to Dallas. Our entertainment budget was limited to bargain movies, and luxuries like vacations were never a consideration.

I was relying on word of mouth and I realized with that approach I really had no chance to succeed in a small market like Abilene. Dallas had no golf club company, of course. The Hogan Company was located in nearby Fort Worth, but they had been through several ownership changes and were not the power of old. At our minuscule size this was a non-issue, but when running a word of mouth campaign it's good not to have many competitors. Thus I made the decision to leave Abilene and move to Dallas. Congruent with the move, I changed the company's name to Adams Golf. At the beginning I just couldn't put my name on the company, because it didn't seem right. But by this time half the people called it "Adams" anyway and I had overcome the self-consciousness.

My wife and I building-shopped during my visits and we found a small place in Richardson, a nice area adjacent to Dallas. We rented some 2,000 square feet in a strip of small businesses. Jackie, her folks, Jack and Jeanette, and my daughter Cindy (who lived in Dallas) did a terrific job of making the place look good, and in October 1991 we moved in.

I remember my high-school football coach telling us in fall practice, "Gentlemen, next weekend is Labor Day, and I promise you, you will labor." He probably got that from his coach who got it from his coach before him, but I still remember it clearly. And moving from Abilene to Dallas on Labor Day 1991 was back-breaking labor. I writhe in pain at the memory.

In the first place, I couldn't part with my "stuff"; it was all I had. That meant two semi-trailers of tables, racks, conveyors, an air compressor big enough to supply air pressure to all of Richardson, and other things that were of little use but weighed a lot. We had contracted the two semi-trucks from Convicts 'R' Us: cash only, they drive, we load. Loading this kind of cargo is normally done with power equipment and skilled people, but we had neither. I'd read someplace that it's important for the leader to set a good example for his team, so I attempted to kill myself by lifting, moving, sliding, and drawing blood in at least five places. And that was just going out. When we arrived in Dallas it started all over again, this time aided by a couple of guys from the labor pool. I don't know how we got everything moved, but somehow we survived, I recovered, and we were now a Dallas company.

I specifically mentioned the labor pool for a reason. One of the guys was James Ezell, at that time of his life not physically or financially in the best of shape, but he was willing to work. We kept James on, taught him the trade of custom club building. We challenged him, compensated him, and today he's an outstanding employee at Adams Golf. That, folks, is one of the best things about starting a business.

I concede that there wasn't much in the story of the first few years to inspire confidence, that would make you want to leave your day job and start off on your own. One of the objectives of this book is to point out the mistakes so that you, the reader, will benefit. The funny part is that I didn't think things were so bad at the time, because I was blinded by my passion for what I was doing. This is a message I've often delivered in talks to entrepreneurs: Don't do it for the money. Do it for a passion, a product, a goal, something that will help you through the bad times, because they *are* coming. The goal of money won't carry you when you hit the physical and emotional pits. There has to be more. Yes, I know, there are really smart people who start up with better plans and faster success rates, but I've done my homework and there are also a lot like me.

I didn't have a job; I had a mission, a place where I had to go every day. It is an understatement to say that it wasn't easy. I never took a sick day. I earned little money. I worked myself to exhaustion in conditions straight out of a Charles Dickens novel and had no life outside of my work. So it's no wonder why I warn people, why I say that people with long years of employment in large companies have a nearly impossible transition trying to make a go of it as an entrepreneurial start-up. I worked so hard because I wanted to. My work became an extension of me, and I couldn't let it down. Was it normal? Of course not. But normal is not on the criteria list. Health is another story. I am a workhorse and in the world of small companies good health is a major asset. It would be an interesting study to compare the overall health of entrepreneurs in start-up environments where getting sick just isn't in any plan.

One thing I know for sure is that the devastating beginning, the loss of my modest funds, became one of my greatest assets. Think about encountering such a sequence of events without passion, and there's no way you'd take another step forward. I hope none of you get to experience that kind of test, but I sincerely hope you'd have the passion to overcome it if you did. I have been asked many times about Adams Golf, and I am I proud that it's an ongoing company doing relatively well. I'm proud of the company, its people, and its reputation, so I smile and bat my eyes in a halo of gratitude. But to tell the truth, I don't think about my success much. I've got ideas I'm working on, and I constantly think about them. That's the nature of the entrepreneurial beast—to always wonder, "Well, what's next?"

I envision myself sitting in this office as head of Barnyard Investments, where would-be entrepreneurs come for advice and, hopefully, funding. If someone walked in with a business plan and proceeded to tell me about their personal life—their wonderful family, two young children, community activities, and so on—they would be in for a disappointment. I do not want to participate in a venture that could ruin a nice, normal existence. I have said in talks that it takes an abnormal, borderline personality to be an entrepreneur, and I still believe that.

TWELVE

BEGINNING THE DALLAS YEARS

As I write this I can imagine the reader thinking, "How did this guy stay in business? What was he selling?" And as I look back, I can honestly say I'm not entirely sure. This is not one of my lame attempts at humor, either. I really have no clear recollection of how I stayed afloat outside of my credit card financing and keeping living costs at a minimum. My eight-year-old car was paid for. I ate, slept, and worked. Sure, we sold product, but not through any specific channels of distribution. We bartered, and somehow we stayed alive.

Concurrent with the move to Dallas I managed to raise some money—$220,000, which I incorrectly figured would last several years. The subject of fundraising will be covered later in the book. It's worthy of a full chapter, if not a whole book itself, and I mention it here to present an accurate position of the company at the time of our move.

I wasn't much of a prospect as a wage earner or a companion since my workdays often exceeded fifteen hours, but in the true mentality of an entrepreneur this was a non-issue to me. I had clubs to build, sales calls to make, a business to develop, a place to go every day that desperately needed my help.

A few months after my move to Dallas (and recovery from the move itself), I drove fifteen miles up the road to visit a project in the works, the Hank Haney Golf Ranch. I had never met Hank and only knew him by reputation as one of the great teachers in golf, but in a weird premonition I saw our relationship being more than casual. A big feature on him in the Sunday edition of the *Dallas Morning News* said he was building the ultimate teaching and practice facility in McKinney, Texas. When I was looking for a place to relocate in Dallas, one of my criteria was that I wanted to be within a reasonable distance of his new facility because I knew we were destined to be a part of each other's futures.

The first time I went to the ranch I was testing a new club theory. It had to do with weight distribution, not just in the head, but throughout the entire club. This was one of the great personal pleasures in my chosen profession. I could come up with an original idea for a golf club, make a sample, and go outside into the warm air to see if it worked. I had no idea if Hank would be there, and wouldn't have known how to approach him if he was.

I loved the place. It wasn't completed yet, but it had a great feel and confirmed my intuition that Hank and I were headed toward some mutual goals. In a later conversation, a mutual acquaintance offered to introduce me to Hank and I gladly accepted. As I remember the first meeting, he was occupied with something involving his facility and his reaction was, "Hello, nice to meet you. I'm very busy." I told him I had an idea that I thought might be of mutual benefit and that I'd like to come back at a more convenient time, and Hank agreed. I know this must sound weird, but I made a couple of future visits looking for the relationship I knew was forthcoming. Not to see if there could be one, but instead to find out what it would be. Soon the plan became obvious.

Hank had acquired an old horse ranch and was in the process of converting it to a golf teaching and practice facility. Years later I was speaking with Tim Cusick (a fine teacher in his own right and now director of instruction at the Four Seasons in Dallas), who had been with Hank from day one. "Hank had a vision," he told me. "It was as clear to him as could be. The old barn would be the indoor facility. Practice range here. Outbuildings remodeled as guest cottages. And let's say, looking at the same landscape, his vision was a little clearer than mine."

In our second meeting I told Hank that I had noticed an unused room in his main building that was big enough to be turned into a repair area and a place to sell Adams Golf clubs, which would provide revenue and more importantly service for his customers. I would do the remodeling. There would be no rent, and in return we would split the profits on repairs. Club sales would go through his operation. Somehow that appealed to him. We shook hands on the deal and it lasted for several years.

In retrospect, I must have I intuited that I had to show him that the arrangement would benefit his customers. He certainly had no concern about growing Adams Golf, nor should he have. I had a different agenda—credibility. Futile attempts to sell my clubs during the Abilene years had taught me that I was out of the golf loop. It wasn't a product issue. I had learned how to make very good clubs, but much of golf equipment sales is based on perception and emotion, driven by excellent marketing. By associating with a reputable name like Hank Haney, I was taking a necessary step toward building my business and its credibility in the marketplace.

We opened the shop in 1992. We had a full-time Adams employee available, and the repair and service end of the business went very well. Adams club sales were a bit slow, though. The truth is, they were nonexistent. At the time we made a full set of woods and irons that were very good, comparable to anything from the major companies and better than some. As we made our sales efforts we heard the same familiar excuses we used to hear back in Abilene. Our clubs were too expensive. They'd never heard of them. We had no marketing, no tour presence—nothing that I hadn't heard before. For some irrational reason I thought that moving our sales location and being associated with a credible name was going to change history. Obviously it didn't, which meant I wasn't using the relationship properly. Again, it was a mindset problem. My idea wasn't wrong. It was a success waiting to happen, and I just needed a little direction.

What followed became the genesis of Adams Golf. This does not mean that the previous years were a waste, because they weren't. I had spent years of trial and error building woods and irons. But by the time I got to the Haney Ranch, the product line was damn good and some of it is still in play to this day. We were getting closer to becoming a real company. We had a few small accounts that believed in us and I knew the ranch presented an opportunity. It just hadn't been correctly identified.

Just Play Better

There is an old saying on the PGA Tour: "Just play better." It's the answer to all problems—money, self-esteem, sponsors, whatever is bugging you. Playing better goes a long way to providing a solution. So it is with starting a business; I've spoken to many entrepreneurs, and often the word "fun" has come up. Whatever we do, we want to have fun doing it. "I left corporate America because it wasn't any fun," they'll tell me. "I want to make sure my people have fun working here." Eventually I'll ask, "Well, what is fun? How do you define it?" I get some pretty diverse answers that range from having good working conditions to great fellow employees, going out for a beer, experiencing freedom in a corporate environment, even tackling new challenges.

Let me tell you what fun is. It's playing better. It's winning the game, and make no mistake, you are in the game of business. I don't care if you have pizza on Tuesdays, or if they let you wear blue jeans on Fridays. I know about good places to work, but at the end of the day it's about success. In a corporation you generally enter into an environment that has history and has experienced success in various forms. Starting up, by definition, is at zero. You are entering the game, and one of the great joys is to experience growing to a successful place in your market. What is that successful place? I don't have any idea, as that will be defined by you and your investors. But you get to establish the culture, and if pizza comes on Tuesday, that's fine as long as your good results are the topic of conversation.

And in fairness, let me add that you can have financial success and be a rotten business. Unhappy employees, high turnover— there's a myriad of symptoms. It's about balance. I know that as the boss you never expect to be loved, because decisions don't always please everyone. But win the game, listen to your employees, work like hell to be fair, and chances are you'll be respected.

Watching someone rise to the occasion is great fun, whether it's management or on a manufacturing line, and I'll say some of my most favorable memories are about employees performing at a high level.

There is a lesson here: if you want your work environment to be more fun, play better.

THIRTEEN

SELLING A SERVICE

*O*ne day, when Hank and I were talking, I told him that his facility was a perfect environment for custom-fitting clubs, and that I was going to design and install an Adams fitting system. Custom-fitted clubs are somewhat analogous to custom clothes, with one major difference. Our bodies all have specific dimensions, but in golf the process of swinging at the ball changes things. Custom clubs must feel comfortable in your hands as you stand up to (address) the ball before you hit it, and also perform during the dynamic motion of the swing itself.

Now, the fact that I didn't have a fitting system at the time was but a minor detail. During my conversation with Hank our destiny became clear to me. This was 1992, and Adams Golf was going to team with Hank Haney to offer golfers custom-designed-and-built clubs. At the time the industry on the whole was following Callaway into the mass-marketing arena. We didn't want to compete there, though, and instead wanted to bring something special to market to attract customers.

It may seem a bit strange talking about Hank in 1992, given his position in the industry today. He is as passionate about teaching the golf swing as I am about making clubs. Today, of course, he's known as Tiger Woods's teacher, and with that comes the recognition associated with the game's greatest player. I will repeat here what I've said many times: I'm a big Tiger Woods fan. I've had the occasion to talk to him very briefly, but I doubt he could pick me out of a lineup. I feel privileged to watch him perform at the incredible level he does and, unlike other sports, I can play in a similar environment and by so doing gain even greater respect for his expertise.

Having spent years with Hank, I can see his teaching in Tiger's swing, and I know better than to enter that arena. I am a club guy, and there is no logical leap from that into the fine-tuning of a golf swing. What I do know is that, regardless of exposure, Hank is as passionate about his efforts today as he was those many years ago. Funny how that characteristic follows successful people.

In a previous chapter I spoke of how, in my early days at the Haney Ranch, I struggled mightily to sell my clubs. Well, one day everything changed. On a Tuesday I couldn't give my clubs away, but on Wednesday I was selling $1,000 sets of custom-fitted irons. They were the same clubs, just altered for the individual. I was no longer selling a product, I was selling a service, and this was one of the greatest, most powerful lessons I've ever learned in business.

Custom-fitting was not new to me. We had done some at Pelz in the "old days," and I had conducted a rather thorough study of the objectives of custom-fitting combined with an analysis of systems currently being used. While equipment had changed and modern analytical tools were available, the objectives in fitting were no different than the earliest recorded efforts. I had one advantage, though, which was my time as a field engineer doing statistical analysis. Incorporating this into the Adams system allowed me to fit people with a high degree of confidence that the clubs would play well in actual usage. The learning process came from the range. I'd measure golfers, build clubs, and give them to the player to be hit. In some cases I made full sets so I could get feedback on use in play. Essentially I was doing a field analysis, not terribly unlike my days at Corning. I was looking for cause-effect relationships, not only on the range but during play. The process evolved into our fitting system, which consisted of fitting clubs and producing a manual covering the procedure. I'm very proud of the system we developed, as it worked then and still does now.

A custom-fitter is part technician and part salesman—not an easy position to fill. Since I had designed the system, I figured I'd better stick around to be sure it performed as advertised. The employee who had worked at the ranch moved away, and I decided to replace him with someone possessing both equipment and fitting knowledge: Me. I worked my "executive job" at Adams from eight until three, and then left for Haney's, where I donned the repair apron and took over as club fitter until they closed at nine. Weekends my schedule was 10:00 A.M. to 10:00 P.M. on Saturday and 1:00 P.M. to 10:00 P.M. on Sunday. I carried orders from the ranch back to our shop, where our three-person crew assembled them. This is my chance to announce that I was a great assembler, but all the shirts I ruined with epoxy and the repeated requests by my crew that I find other things to do proved otherwise. Good assemblers are dexterous, patient, and meticulous, and I was none of the above. My goals were speed and accuracy, and if the work area looked like a tornado path, that was the price.

I had helped out at the ranch before, so the "before-fitting" process of just club repair was familiar, which only made the jump in sales such an amazing revelation. I experienced the phenomenon of not being able to sell a thing, and then offering the same product custom-fitted and signing people up for fitting sessions. It was even more dramatic than that. When people bought, half the time they didn't ask the price and when they did no one haggled. They just wanted to know how soon they could get their clubs. They did more than buy, too. They brought their friends back, called others, and stayed in touch, some to this day. I wasn't just selling product—I was building customers. I cannot emphasize the transformation enough; I never look at a product today without asking myself what service is being sold.

The change to selling a service did much more than provide a modest boost to our sales. It exposed me to the greatest possible environment where I could learn to make playable golf clubs for all skill levels. Remember the old days when I was a field engineer tracking sophisticated glass products into customer facilities and monitoring performance? All I did was trade that environment for the driving range, where I tracked club performance. But it was more than that. Golf balls don't really do too much. They just kind of lie around, and then a force whacks them in some direction. That might sound pretty stupid, but from an analytical basis it's perfect. I watched and measured, took data. Since I had my little shop right there, I could make clubs of different characteristics and have golfers of all skill levels try them. And in doing so, I learned that my service wasn't really custom fitting clubs, but providing better ball flight. This is selling a service defined. After all, what good are custom clubs if they don't improve the flight of the golf ball?

My little shop not only served as the center for Adams custom fitting, it became my personal R&D center. I had developed a formula I called "goop," a mixture of tungsten powder and epoxy. The procedure was to drill holes in various locations on club heads and fill them with goop, looking to see if the resultant weight redistribution affected ball flight. It was a far cry from the sophisticated processes used today, but by tying my experiments directly to ball flight I came close to achieving optimum design.

There were golfers of all skill levels at the ranch. They didn't know they were my personal testers, and fortunately they were willing to hit the clubs I carried out to the range. One time my goal was to design a one-iron that was easy to hit, so I put all the goop in the bottom of the club, lowering the center of gravity, and had girls from the local high-school team serve as my testers. My thinking was that their swing speeds would be slow but the swings themselves decent, so I was testing in a fairly repetitive environment. The club actually worked pretty well and I stored the knowledge. While I didn't realize it at the time, it would eventually be used on a later product.

Selling a Service

I used to conduct seminars for specialty golf retail and pro shops, and always started off with the same question: "How many here sell golf clubs?" Of course, all of the hands would go up. Then I'd tell them, "Go home. You have no chance for success." If you are only selling a product, a commodity, then as the consumer it's my job to find the lowest price. After all, you just told me the product is the sale, not a service.

Further, who is your competition? Only everyone, from every possible retail outlet to the Internet. You as the selling person are unimportant. I could replace you with a machine, or a chimp for that matter.

Now take the exact same product and sell it as a service. Take something as simple as a sand wedge. "Oh, Mr. Balata, I see you're looking at sand wedges. Where do you play? Yes, I've played there; nice course, and they have some serious traps. Did you know that when we tested these wedges, we found that these two models worked best out of that kind of sand?"

Look at what I've just done. I've taken a relatively simple selling environment and added my expertise, with no sales pressure whatsoever. Unless Mr. Balata is in the top one percent in the category of equipment knowledge, my service is going to be very powerful. What am I selling? Better performance. Furthermore, if I'm right, he now recognizes me for my expertise. He comes back to buy more, and he tells his friends about me. When Callaway was selling a truckload of Big Bertha drivers a day, they were doing it at $400 a club, unheard-of in golf history. And the reason why Callaway was able to charge $400 a pop was that they weren't selling a club, but a service: More distance off the tee, the heart and soul of golfers' dreams.

Do not confuse this with *customer* service. Many companies still try to sell a product and think that by providing good customer service they understand the objective. But that's a backwards way of thinking. If you do the job correctly in the first place, pay attention to your customer, and focus on making it a WOW experience for them, customer service isn't really necessary.

To management, especially the guys with Title-itis, I say, "Have you ever considered a goal that makes customer service calls unnecessary?" I don't mean inquiries about the company, either. I mean the daily screw-ups. Recently, an online company completely messed up my order. I had filled out all their requests properly, which they acknowledged. I finally ended up speaking to a very nice and contrite lady who said, "What can I do to make this right for you?" She was so nice I didn't give her the answer I wanted to, which was just to do the job right in the first place so I wouldn't have to spend time getting things right afterwards. I really don't want *anything*, just what I ordered. That's why my advice to management is, "Close the crutch department and concentrate on making your customer's experience a WOW from the beginning."

Ask yourself what service you will be providing your customer. If it's something tangible, what will it bring to the party that makes it desirable? I tell retailers that their real business is to create customers, to create an environment in which your shoppers become your ads, where they tell their friends about the great experience they had. Price cannot be completely ignored, but reduce the buying decision to price only and you'll have a million competitors. Focus on selling a service and your only competition is those who do that better than you.

Want an example in the most competitive of industries, where everyone sells exactly the same product? Take Florida's Publix Supermarkets. Their motto is "Where Shopping is a Pleasure," and for generations they have been one of the most successful grocery chains in America. They sell the same groceries as everyone else, but have managed to convey that it isn't just about the products, it's about the customer.

I'll be even more specific. Their stores are in Florida. It's warm there, so people wear shorts and light clothing. Many years ago, customers in the frozen foods section would get goosebumps, so Publix decided to put doors on their refrigerated cases. Even though they were criticized for the expense, it was worth it to benefit their customers. Then along came the energy crisis, and guess who ended up saving money by containing the cold air?

FOURTEEN

TAKING MY SHOW ON THE ROAD

My main function at Adams in those early days was to serve as its sales department. The Haney Ranch was our only fitting center and, though it contributed more than 90 percent of our total sales, it simply wasn't enough. I wanted to take my fitting show on the road, but it was hard to call prospective customers and say, "Hi. You don't know who I am, but I'd like to come to your club and custom fit your members." Not surprisingly, I did not elicit a great response. In fact, I received no response at all, so I decided it was time to add marketing to the mix. Of course, I had no money for marketing, which added further difficulty to the equation.

Hank had instituted a program called "Teaching the Teacher," in which twenty to thirty-five top club pros from around the country would come to his ranch for a three-day seminar. The seminar focused on helping these club pros become better teachers, and those who attended received education credit, which PGA club professionals need to maintain their rankings. I approached Hank and suggested that as an "opening act," I could conduct a seminar on golf equipment and custom-fitting. It would not be a sales pitch for Adams, just an informative session on equipment in general. I suspected that the type of golf pro willing to attend a program like Hank's would be interested in the vagaries of golf equipment. Hank agreed to give it a try, although I noticed that my first presentation was well-attended by his staff. I'd like to think they all wanted to hear me speak, but I suspect there was a bit of monitoring going on as well.

I did keep my word to Hank about not plugging Adams, but I let it slip out that I was available to come to their clubs to conduct fitting days, and the response I received was positive. This was early spring of 1993 and I scheduled bookings for the summer, so I only had a short time to find a replacement at the ranch before I took my show on the road.

Asking around, I found a perfect guy to take my place at the Haney Ranch. Max Puglielli had considerable experience in club-fitting and club-building. What made him so desirable was that he had the same passion, the same desire for excellence, that I did. He still has it to this day, as he is now in charge of our tour staff. I cannot count the number of times Champions Tour players have gone out of their way to specifically single out Max as the best tour representative they have ever worked with. Drawing a description of a small company employee who gave me enthusiasm would produce a picture of Max.

There was one obstacle to hiring Max back then, and that was salary. It wasn't that his request was outrageous. It was quite reasonable, actually, but it meant that I had to take a pay cut so we could afford him, and it still increased our overhead. Taking him on meant we had to improve. We were still a three-horse race and were hiring a thoroughbred.

With the pressure of Max's salary added to our massive overhead, I undertook the job of increasing sales. Following up on leads from the seminars, I took my act on the road and, for the better part of the next two years, I became a one-man sales force conducting fitting sessions on public driving ranges, public and private golf courses, and resorts. I've mowed the grass on the ends of ranges because it was too high to hit balls, fit clubs in hundred-degree temperatures and freezing winds. I've fit beginners, great players, and everything in between. This provided sales for Adams Golf and just about destroyed my aging body. Fitting clubs requires carrying two large golf bags plus fitting accessories. Add clothes and personal items, and you can imagine how difficult it was to get around. Still, I pressed on, booking the cheapest possible travel and lodging accommodations I could as I trekked across the country (actually three countries before I was done). Saturday night stay-overs were automatic. Valujet, Sunjet, any jet that was trying to build customers at bargain prices got my business. I rented cars from Tiny Cars 'R' Us, stayed in paper-thin motels, and loved every minute of it. We were adding more customers, I was learning with every experience, and our business was growing. We had turned the corner.

Well, not exactly. In 1994, sensing great things were on the horizon, I took our books to a CPA for an audit. I was the primary bookkeeper back then, which meant that I kept a green pad in which I entered sales, expenses, and all the important stuff. I also was helped greatly by Patty Walsh, who started part-time in 1991 and came on full-time shortly thereafter. I'm a great admirer of employees like Patty, Max Puglielli, and Ann Neff, who came on board early and stuck with me during those long periods of week-to-week existence. None of us had titles, but we did what was necessary to keep the company afloat.

I collected our 1994 books and our historical financial records and took them to the CPA. He called me when he was finished and told me that, much to his surprise, everything was in pretty good order, so I went over to retrieve them. They were sitting on his receptionist's desk with a cover letter, which was a statement concerning our ability (or lack thereof) to stay in business. I confronted him about it and he told me it was his professional duty to provide a going concern letter if an audit indicated serious trouble. I was furious and couldn't think of anything to say, so I blurted out, "The hell with you. That was my best year!"

Around that time I hired another key employee, Richard (Dick) Murtland. Dick and I had gone to college together at Clarkson and both attended for the same reason: financial aid. Dick played baseball and I played basketball. This was the late 1950s to early '60s and our teams were lousy, but we contributed. The school was very hard and had a high attrition rate. Students had to find ways to relieve the stress, and Dick and I often ended up in the same places for R&R. Somehow we managed to graduate without one honor between us. More importantly, we both got jobs, which was the main reason for attending college in the first place. We went our separate ways, staying in touch occasionally, and in 1994 I got a call from Dick, saying, "I'm in town. Let's have dinner."

At dinner we filled each other in on the past thirty-five years in typical male fashion, taking about twenty minutes to do the job. He then told me he was going to take early retirement from ARCO, where he had worked in the international division as a manager for the past ten years. When I asked him what was next for him, he told me he had no plans beyond the need to do something. What followed was right out of the entrepreneurs' handbook. I offered him a job, telling him that I needed someone to run operations while I ran around the country trying to increase sales. I offered him a nice VP title and a desk, but the job had one drawback: no pay. The best I could do was fix him up with free range balls at the Haney Ranch, get him at least ten free lessons, and whenever we went to lunch I promised to pay.

I also supplemented my offer with stock in the company, and after taking a day to think it over he accepted the position. For over three years Dick worked full-time and was never paid a nickel. He got his range balls and the occasional lunch. He got one more benefit, too. When we went public he enjoyed a wonderful payday, enough to retire again a couple of years later, this time for good.

FIFTEEN

THE WORLD OF FUNDRAISING

As our little business started to take shape it wasn't just me any more, and I knew I needed to raise money to take advantage of some of the opportunities that came our way. I'd read books on raising money, had worked closely with the venture community in Silicon Valley, and had learned that one thing is absolute: fundraising is the key job of the entrepreneur. Until that's accomplished, more time will be spent raising money (or worrying about it) than any other issue. If there were a book titled *The Guaranteed Fundraising System for Small Businesses*, it would be a bestseller. The only problem is that it would be a lie, as there is no guaranteed method. Furthermore, most entrepreneurs hate raising money, and I was no exception. You go out, sell your soul, and seldom get positive results. Failure in itself is not the worst part of the process. It's the vulnerability that makes for discouraging times.

The best, almost surefire way to raise money is to have a great track record. If you've raised money before and multiplied that into a successful return, the investors will come to you. If you don't have that kind of track record, perhaps you can bring someone into your team who does. If your product is really good, you can give a nice piece of the action to a player in return for bringing funding to the party. Remember, the name of the game is to win, and you *can* hold on to a good thing until it dies.

If you do not have a great track record or the ability to bring someone into your fold who does, you can go about fundraising the way I did: the hard way, hat in hand, chasing every lead and hating every minute of it. There's an old vaudeville skit about a guy who goes to his neighbor's house to borrow a lawnmower. On the way over he starts talking to himself, thinking of all the different reasons why his neighbor will refuse him. By the time he gets to his neighbor's door he says, "Keep the damn mower, I didn't want it anyway." That was kind of like me raising money.

My first funding was similar to that of many small companies in that it was backed by friends. A bunch of golf buddies from Silicon Valley and my brother Steve got together and funded me with $220,000. This was a few years after my inauspicious beginning. I had somehow survived and was preparing to move to Dallas. At the time I thought I'd never need another dime, which only shows how naïve I was. The money lasted a couple of years, but as noted earlier I wasn't setting the sales world on fire and things were getting grim. The Silicon Valley economy was in one of its down cycles, so going back to my original group for more financing was out of the question.

I was preparing for the 1993 PGA Merchandise Show (preparing to drop out, really) when the subject of money came up in a conversation with a customer. Sensing my plight (okay, I told him) he said, "I didn't know you were looking for money. I think you make great stuff. I'd like to invest in your company." He might have said more, but I never would have heard it, as his magic words obliterated all else.

With the backing of my new investor, the pressure was off and I made my preparations for the upcoming show (we were to get together after the show and work out the actual amount and valuation). As in previous years I drove my booth down, displayed my wares to little fanfare, and drove back. Significant show sales were not forthcoming in 1993 but show expenses were, and I had no money to cover the bills, so I eagerly sought out my new investor upon returning to Dallas. I had difficulty connecting with him over the phone and when I drove by his business he was tied up. I was due at the Haney Ranch and happened to run into Hank when I arrived. He inquired about the show, and somehow in the conversation the name of my new investor came up. "*That* guy," interrupted Hank. "He came out here, told me he wanted to invest. I spent days with him and then he disappeared. Not a dime."

The sound next heard was that of my hopes crashing. I needed the money badly, and Hank's little anecdote told the story. I left a clear message at my "investor's" business about needing to follow up on our conversation before the show, but a reply was not forthcoming. In fact, he hasn't returned my call to this day. I was really depressed. Things had been bad before, but we were farther along this time. The monthly nut was greater and the piece of me invested was greater. Then the phone rang.

"Hi, Barney. It's Clyde Smith. How have you been?" Smitty was an old friend dating back to my grocery days. He had developed a tremendously successful chain of superstores in Phoenix, which he had sold, and was now living in the Hill Country in Central Texas. I knew he was aware of my efforts, yet we did not communicate regularly and I had not approached him for any money.

"Peggy [his wife] and I are calling from Hawaii. We have a little year-end money to invest and thought of you. Are you open to investors?" I managed to mumble that something could be easily worked out, and we agreed that I would drive over to a small town bank in Texas where he did business and pick up a cashier's check. There was no discussion of valuation, no due diligence, no market studies or business plan, just faith. And driving over to the bank, I didn't know the amount. By this time I was so scared, so traumatized by my previous fundraising failures, that I didn't have the courage to ask "How much?" I set out immediately for the bank and took my miniature schnauzer with me. I guess I figured that if I failed again, at least my dog would still love me.

Arriving at the bank, I was introduced to an officer who handed me a check for $230,000. I have a copy of it to this day. There is nothing else to say about it. Clyde and Peggy made a choice to invest in me, and for whatever reason it was that prompted their decision I am eternally grateful.

I was determined not to get so far behind financially again, so along with my day and evening jobs I concentrated more on raising money. Let me tell you a couple of things not to do. Everyone who offers to raise money for an up-front fee should get the same answer: no. You are desperate, and *every* penny is needed to run the business. If this person can raise money, he or she can take a fair fee once the task is accomplished. I've researched this one, and the results are universal. Never pay anyone anything up front.

Enter the scams. When you're desperate for money, you're vulnerable. I don't look at them anymore, but there are ads in major newspapers that offer, "Money to invest. Call this number." You answer an ad and "they" contact you. "They" are very reputable-sounding, having access to offshore money. The source can't be revealed, of course, but generally it's South American or Middle Eastern. You are not concerned, you say. You are legit, and if critical funds come from a questionable source, it wouldn't be the first time in business history.

In my last encounter, "they" sent me a very official-looking set of documents with a legal style heading. The documents requested just enough information to appear legitimate, but not so much that I'd be discouraged. Within a few days I received a call telling me that I had not only been approved, but for an amount greater than I requested, and that there was no up-front fee. Instead, a percentage would be due upon my receipt of the money. Now is *that* the answer to your prayers or what? Never mind that their due diligence must have taken five or ten minutes, or that their source is mysteriously secret. This is about money. When you are in serious need you do not think rationally.

A few days after my congratulatory phone call, an agent called back to explain the logistics. I would be getting the money (more than $4 million if I remember correctly) in a few days. Because the money was offshore there would be processing fees, some $50,000, and they wanted to be clear that these were expenses, not a fee to them. Being of great wisdom and experience I asked for a reference, a happy customer. Without losing a beat the agent told me their system was founded on confidentiality and that upon receiving the funds I would be treated accordingly. I told them I'd have to work on getting the transaction fee money and would call back in two days.

I waited, and four days later they called me with a high-pressure ultimatum. The offshore money had to be moved, they said, and if I didn't act they would have to go to the next company. I said that $50,000 was too rich and asked if they'd be willing to accept $25,000 instead. There was a pause, and then the agent said they would make a one-time exception for me. I then asked one more question. If the $4 million would be forthcoming in two or three days, rather than pay $25,000 now, why not wait until I got the money and they could withhold the entire $50,000 that they originally wanted? Not fair, they said. They had done hundreds of these transactions and it wouldn't be fair to their previous customers to change the rules for me. I told them I'd call back the next day and I did, telling them that my brother, who lived in their city, would hand-deliver the check. They said that this was fine and that they'd call back with a meeting place. I then told them my brother was very happy for me, that he worked in the Federal prosecutor's office, and that he was glad that this time I had done my homework and was dealing with good people. I didn't want to antagonize these guys. They had my address and were crooks, so I tried to sound as sincere and as dumb as I could. And like that first guy who sent me to the PGA show, they never called back. A few days later I tried their number, only to find that it was no longer working.

Did I invent this story to add a little intrigue to the book? No way. Did I ever read about these little adventures so I'd be forewarned? I certainly didn't. That scam was just one of several I encountered. If you think I'm just gullible, I can tell you about a recent story I read in the paper in which a well-educated, experienced businessman spent hundreds of thousands of his own money on a "fundraiser" with access to offshore money who never delivered, or about a friend who flew to Europe to secure funding from a mysterious source and returned home one more fee short. In short, scams work.

All of the money I raised came from people I was introduced to who bought into my passion. Friends Don Hall and Rod Grettler introduced me to the folks at Royal Oil and Gas in Indiana, Pennsylvania, and got me a meeting with them. In my cost-conscious style, my motel was not of the five-star variety and my room had no heat, so I presented myself the next morning to Steve Patchin and Paul Brown of Royal deprived of any sleep. They signed on and ultimately became my biggest investor. And you know why? Because something happened that wasn't definable: they believed in me. There was no real plan, no forecast, and it went that way every time with every investor.

I was given the name of Roland Casati, an extremely successful real estate man from Chicago who had been an early investor in Callaway. When I met with him in Palm Desert, he told me my timing was poor relative to his investment cycle. A few months later he called me in Texas and told me he had decided to invest. I asked if he wanted to see the business plan and he said no, he was investing in me, buying into my passion. I'll repeat what I wrote earlier: I have no foolproof formula for raising money. But I do know that you have to follow every lead, and work at least as hard as you do in your business. If someone isn't interested, maybe they know someone who is. No lead is too small to ignore.

These people constituted my investor group. I've spoken to several entrepreneur organizations and it's surprising how similar the stories are (even the scams). Yes, some entrepreneurial businesses have angel investors who specialize in small companies, generally in the local geographic area. Often customers who believe in the product become investors. The stories are legion and there are several books on the subject. One thing is constant. For the entrepreneur it's a painful process. There are an amazing number of people who will lead you astray, promising and not delivering. Who knows what psychological malfunction drives them? There are countless scam artists out there, and when it comes to fundraising I can give this summary: If it just seems too good to be true, it is. If it costs you one dime up front, run and hide. And you'll work harder raising money than you ever dreamed.

How Necessary Is a Business Plan When Raising Funds?

Buy any book on fundraising and the business plan will be put forth as a significant, if not critical, tool. I guess it is, but I never raised a dime off my business plan. Yes, I had one—a good one, too. I spent days on the critical executive summary, the part the real investors read before they turn the rest over to their staff to analyze. I still have my plan. I reread it when researching this book, and it's still good. But it never mattered. Since I've never raised money for any business but my own, I can report that it came down to investors' analysis of me. This is not some ego trip. It's how four different and significant groups made their decisions. A business plan helps you with your objectives in that it can identify markets and show what percentage you must sell to be successful. It can do a lot of things, including be an anchor.

Often a project starts out with a six-cylinder engine heading down a highway, and halfway there you realize that a four-cylinder ATV headed for unpaved road will get you in the market faster, and will ultimately help the highway vehicle. The only problem is that you sold your investors on a highway business plan and this major change wasn't foreseen. Further, it requires more cash, so now you have to go back to your investors and say, "Ah, remember that plan, that beautiful Word document with all the charts and market share figures? We have a little change." Or, you can avoid this displeasure by sticking to the original plan and underperforming. Most business plans go out three to five years, which is generally hilarious, as companies that are in established industries struggle with accurate plans beyond a year. A business plan has general value in that it helps map things out a bit. But do not wear your business plan around your neck like a millstone.

Over the years I've told my fundraising stories in a variety of entrepreneurial environments. Without fail, afterwards someone will come up and say, " You think you have stories? Let me tell you about *my* experiences raising money."

SIXTEEN

THE ORIGIN OF THE TIGHT LIES CLUB

In 1994, when Max Puglielli replaced me as the club fitter at the Haney Ranch, I was able to take the custom-fitting process on the road, which was essential for increasing sales. During my travels I constantly analyzed my customers to determine how could I do a better job serving them. As I thought more about the concept, I realized that while my service was custom clubs, the goal was better ball flight. There was no question that custom clubs were the vehicle but, if my customers could have improved ball flight by taking mud baths, I would have been in the towel business. Once I started thinking along those lines, I asked myself what constituted better ball flight, and one thought struck me that is still a cornerstone of Adams Golf today: ease of playability.

My job was to make it as easy as possible to hit enjoyable shots. There was one particular area where I was failing (along with everybody else), and that was the long shot played to the green with the ball on the ground. Furthermore, when I asked my customers where I could be of the greatest help to them, guess which was their major area of concern. At the time the golf industry was in the "oversize revolution." Driver heads were large and getting larger and, as part of a matched set, fairway woods were following right along. Given a deep-face fairway wood with the ball on the ground, most golfers did not perform well.

I had essentially the same set makeup as everyone else did, but the clubs weren't right for the job and it wasn't until I started thinking in terms of ball flight that I realized my dilemma. Customers would come in for a fitting and I'd do a great job with the clubs, but the problem was that there were areas where I had optimized the fitting but not optimized the customers' ball flight, and that's not providing customer service at the highest level. Identifying the problem, I started thinking in terms of a solution. It wasn't an immediate process, and while driving home at night I would process all the designs I'd tried and conversations I'd held, accessing my data bank in search of an answer.

The phrase "optimized ball flight" sounds good if you say it fast, but what is it? The answer is not universal. The help you'd give to Grandpa Barney and his 82-mile-per-hour swing speed doesn't relate to his son Eddie, who can hit one-irons over a building. Being somewhat selfish, I concentrated on Grandpa's issues.

I remember a conversation I had with Curt Siegel, the longtime pro at Laurel Valley in Pennsylvania. I was there with a friend, and in a casual conversation Curt remarked that the fairways were being cut so short it was harder and harder for his members to get longer shots airborne, and that maybe a special club was needed. As I became aware of the situation it seemed that I had stumbled on an epidemic. It's kind of like looking for cars. When you're not in the market, cars are cars. But when you're thinking of buying, every car on the road is of interest, and so it was with me and fairway woods.

I remembered something I had read in a book on golf and equipment by Gene Sarazen. He described how he thought a fairway wood should look. He wanted to see the top of the ball higher than the top of the club face so it would appear easy to get airborne. Finally, after months of this random process of collecting data, one evening I was helping at the ranch and did not go straight home. Instead I went back to the shop.

I'd like to say that I opened my computer and started working on a sophisticated design program right away. Two things would be missing from that equation, though: a computer (which I did not own), and a clue about what one did. After all, this was eons ago, early 1995, and even if some prankster had put a computer on my desk I wouldn't have known how to turn it on, much less operate a sophisticated design program. I was familiar with a slide rule, but for technical tools let's just say I didn't measure up. So instead, I reached for one of the great inventions of all mankind—the yellow pad.

I started sketching a head design that I felt would help me provide more service to my customers. As much as I'd like to write that the entire business and marketing plan for the Tight Lies unfolded as I sat there, I can't. What I did was imagine the circumstances in which my customers were having problems, and by that I specifically mean the golf ball on the ground. Then I visualized the club hitting the ball and thought of what I could do to improve results. I didn't think in terms of the head, but in terms of the head and ball coming into contact.

As I visualized the ball-club contact, a club shape started to form in my mind. I knew the initial objective was to get the ball into the air, but the task was much more complex than that. While getting airborne was a good start, the ball also had to go forward, preferably somewhere in the direction of the target. It was also important that the club I'd be putting into the golfer's hand instill a sense of confidence and fun. Easier said than done.

I won't go into the specifics of the design characteristics here, because this is more about the process than the engineering. A good friend of mine, Mickey Newbury, was a great songwriter who sadly is no longer with us. One time I asked him how he wrote a song. He looked at me and said, "Barnyard, it's all in there," pointing at his head. "Sometimes it just comes out." I've been asked how I designed the Tight Lies given the absence of any computer assistance, and Mickey's answer is as close as I can come. What I did was think of all the clubs I knew hit well with the ball on the ground, and applied whatever characteristics I thought would make this design work. It really was as simple as that.

For the previous ten years or more, I had been totally immersed in designing, testing, and making clubs. Although they achieved little to no commercial success, I had still accumulated a wealth of data. Then, to top it off, I had spent the last three years on the range with golfers of all skill levels and attitudes playing in myriad conditions. I include attitudes here because they're critical to a golfer's success.

Big companies with large marketing budgets can get people to play their products partially through the sheer force of their marketing. But I knew that if I came up with a club to help golfers, getting them to try it would be a challenge. Most golfers realize they aren't great players and don't want to put themselves in a position where they'll be embarrassed. So if I'm going to present a different product, it has to first pass what ultimately became known as the "weird test." The club can be different, but not so much that it evokes remarks like, "My gosh, Harry, has your game gotten so bad that you'll play with that? It looks like a toilet plunger." Now, Harry may love the club, but sooner or later he will hit some bad shots with it, take grief from his pals, lose confidence, and then what we have is another club for the garage.

As I was sketching out the design of this club I wrote down the name Tight Lies, which came from the visualization of the golf ball lying on closely cut grass, known in golf terminology as a tight lie. The name and the club just seemed to work together, so when I had my first samples made that was the name I used on the club.

The process of naming a golf club (or, I assume, any consumer product) is very difficult, and there are entire companies that do naming as a business. You have to be very careful and follow a legal procedure so that you don't end up using a name owned by someone else. I didn't realize it at the time, but the fact that Tight Lies was available as a name was a sign.

There are usage rights, meaning that the name is common to everyone, and you can use it but so can everyone else. But none of those thoughts entered my head because I was focused on trying to make a golf club. I completed my sketch with the Tight Lies name and faxed it to my supplier in Taiwan. Two days later I got a fax back saying that they had serious questions about the design and suggested some changes. These people were very good and had club-design experience with U.S. and Japanese companies. I valued their input, but was insistent that I wanted it as sketched.

Today when a club is designed, it does come from very sophisticated computer systems, and the design isn't stand-alone. Each dimension of the head is referenced and cross-checked by a large database. Wax samples are now made in hours so the visual aspects can be reviewed before tooling, and even with all that design and preparation, first samples are rarely indicative of the final product.

My yellow pad process was so casual that it screamed redesign, yet I wanted it done exactly as presented with no more technical certainty than a gut feeling that I was right. As I look back now with a greater knowledge of the technical aspects of club design, it's almost spooky. I convinced my supplier to follow the original sketch and started the six- to eight-week waiting period for samples by going back to my world of custom fitting and fundraising.

When the heads finally arrived, I installed shafts and grips and headed to the ultimate test lab—the range. The first shot with this new design convinced me I was right. It performed exactly as I had planned. I then started a test process consisting of giving the club to golfers on the range and asking for their reaction. Here's the part where I write about success, the thrill of designing something and watching your customers turn to you with teary-eyed looks of gratitude. Except that wasn't the reaction, at least not the complete one.

SEVENTEEN

THE WOW TEST

*T*he first thing that happened when the club was tested on the range was the WOW result, which meant that I'd hear testers remarking, "WOW, that really hits good." I found this reaction so critical that it became one of the driving forces behind the entire Adams Golf business culture, and I'm proud to say that it's still alive at Adams today.

What is a WOW reaction? Personally, it's very powerful. It's intuitive, and that means it's influenced by everything in my personal data bank. WOW, that tastes great, drives nice, looks outstanding. I could go on, but in its simplicity it says everything.

When I analyzed initial response I began to understand the power of the WOW, the pure gut response versus something I'll call pre-influenced. Isn't that what marketing is all about, to precondition the user to have a WOW response, or at least make them think they will, so they'll buy? In my case, on the range, potential customers were not only skeptical, they were preconditioned *not* to like the club. The major brands all sold fairway woods and, being oversized, they were the opposite look of the Tight Lies. These big companies augmented their position with millions of dollars in advertising and marketing. Adams was at best a no-name.

Furthermore, my customers were preconditioned by what they saw the pros on tour using, and also by the most powerful influence of all—peer usage. So there were certain hurdles of perception and skepticism to overcome. And to be honest, not everyone loved the club when they first saw it. Most of the testers did, though, and I'll forever remember all the times I heard, "WOW, this is pretty good."

Some customers vigorously defended their own clubs even when the Tight Lies' ball flight proved more effective. This latter phenomenon marked another lesson that I carry with me to this day, and it's about the power of branding. I have participated in countless demo days over the years. For you readers who are not golfers, a demo day is like golf's version of a street fair. Held either at a golf course or a public range, organizers bring in several companies that set up tents with hitting areas in the front. The golfers go from tent to tent hitting drivers, irons, or whatever their interest is. If you are one of the big-name brands you generally get a spot in the center, and the smaller companies set up toward the ends.

When a golfer came to my tent, my objective was to show him that our clubs produced better shots with less effort. Some of the other tent minders were employees. Some of them really worked hard, while others were just going through the motions. I was serious. These were *my* clubs and I knew they were good. This made accepting the frequent defeats very difficult. Golfers would hit our product well, even better than the others, but then turn away to buy something else. And it was all about brand recognition.

All amateur golfers fight insecurity. We all miss shots. And buying a new driver or fairway wood from a well-known, strongly advertised company provides a certain degree of comfort. But to buy from the enthusiastic guy at the end of the range means that the product has to be truly outstanding. Not good, but outstanding.

Fighting against the various "big guys" in the years that followed, I became very experienced with rejection. This is not unusual, but in fact the norm. For every small company that gets quick acceptance there are about a zillion that suffer years of rejection. Whether golfers or industry experts, these people were expressing their honest opinion of our product, and they came from a variety of sources. Who was I to tell them they were all wrong? But it wasn't about me, it was about the WOW test. If I hadn't experienced it firsthand and seen the reaction from customers, the Tight Lies never would have become a marketed product. But I did see it, and this is why I consider the WOW test to have such a compelling influence on everything I do.

Did I stride confidently through the sea of praise and criticism? Not exactly. It was more like a fighter getting hit constantly. He's not sure where the next punch is coming from, but he knows that it is coming. He's also been hit enough to know he can take the blow. As an example, I was concerned that the name Tight Lies would identify the club as a specific utility club, good for getting out of trouble. I designed it for all fairway applications and didn't want my customers to have any reservations, so I changed the name to HT Fairway, the HT standing for high trajectory. I actually had samples made. I didn't keep any, but if anyone finds one it might have a collector's value, like a stamp with a mistake.

I was pretty proud of my change and took some clubs to the Haney Golf Ranch. On the range practicing was Rocky Thompson, a colorful character who also happened to be a very fine player then competing on the Senior Tour. Rocky had hit the Tight Lies and appreciated the design. When I walked onto the range I had some clubs with me and he inquired if they were another design. I said, "No, I just decided to change the name," and showed him the new artwork. Rocky responded by telling me I was crazy.."Tight Lies is one of the greatest names I ever heard for a golf club," he said. "Changing it is a purely dumb idea." Did I explain my position, justify the name change, show him my market study? No. I did none of the above. Instead I turned, went into the shop, called my office, and had them fax my supplier that I was changing the name back. Yes sir, I was one confident guy with a handle on all the details.

A Rose by Any Other Name...

If your product is name-dependant, you can spend a lot of time and money looking for the perfect name. My clubs are called Adams for a fairly obvious reason, and I have twice been served with legal notice that I can't use the name. One of these led me to a real deposition a few years back in which I was asked, "Where did you get the idea to use Adams on your clubs?" My answer? "Probably my birth certificate."

Moreover, if you get started with a product and achieve a little publicity, wait until you export and find someone who has read about your success, registered the name in that country, and would be only too happy to sell it back to you. At that juncture you may respond as I did, full of indignity at such a cheap rip-off, only to learn that the legal costs of defending your position exceed the buyback price. This is no coincidence.

This is an area where a modest investment in legal guidance can save you a lot of grief down the road. Even then, any attorney will tell you that, until tested in court, nothing is for sure. It's pretty easy to fall in love with a name, but remember that it will only be worthwhile if you market it properly. Names like Xerox and Kodak sound like answers to a Scrabble quiz without millions in advertising and consumer education. You can spend a lot of time and money searching for the perfect name, but I'd save the dough for marketing.

EIGHTEEN

TIGHT LIES—THE REAL BEGINNING

I'm no marketing genius. I'm a club-fitter who needed a tool to do a better job. After my design proved worthy I proceeded to integrate it into my fitting system. Case closed. Except it wasn't. In fact it was just beginning to open.

We had only one phone in our building at the time, which was fine because nobody ever called, especially not customers. But after a few weeks of testing the Tight Lies we started getting calls, and they all had a familiar theme. The caller would say, "I played with Bubba the other day and he hit this shot on number fourteen over the trees on the green, and I know he ain't that good. He showed me his club. I think it's called tight shots or something, and he said you make them. Is that true?" And in a hundred variations that was the call, a new experience for us.

This was fall of 1995, and after being figuratively hit over the head with the phone calls, I had the thought that maybe we had a product that had stand-alone sales potential. The problem was that I didn't know what to do.

In the early days of Adams I tried selling into the specialty golf retail environment and learned I had no chance. Regardless of some local success, there was no demand from the normal distribution channels. If we tried, they wouldn't give us a meeting. Let me add that this is no failure on their part, because retailers don't just buy product. They buy a combination of product, marketing, and sales support. We had one of the three, and they wouldn't have even agreed with that.

One of my fitting customers and I had talked about him coming to work for us in a sales position. Mark Gonsalves was a fine player with sales experience and some exposure to the golf industry. I was looking for someone outside the industry. I had been in a long time and knew the traditional approaches. I didn't feel we could take the traditional route and believed that instead we had to look for a unique plan.

I hired Mark as VP of sales and gave him the task of looking for a new distribution approach. I told him to look around, look at other industries; to use a now-clichéd phrase, to think outside the box. He did just that, and the first approach we actually tried (as opposed to discussed) was direct sales. I don't remember the exact numbers, but he found a highly successful midwestern direct-mail company that had millions of names and mailed an incredible number of pages each month featuring special products. These guys were very sophisticated, to the point where a few days after a mailing they could analyze results and predict sales within tenths of a percent.

In our case it was even more accurate. When we convinced them to send a mailer to over ten thousand proven golf equipment consumers, it produced zero sales. Zip. Nada. And the forecast matched. This was a bit of a letdown, but for us it just meant we needed to try something else, because we knew we had the WOW experience.

Then Mark came back with "the answer." He told me we were going to sell the clubs over the phone. I was mortified. "You mean like those telemarketers who call me in the middle of dinner?" I asked. "No way!" But then a significant moment in our company's history occurred. Mark had done his homework, showing me studies where telemarketing succeeded for some well-known companies. Furthermore, we wouldn't be doing telemarketing as I knew it; this was telesales, calling only on the established golf distribution channels. Mark had found a guy by the name of Ric Jarrett who had extensive experience using this approach, and together they were going to market the Tight Lies. I call this a significant moment because it was one of the first times I relinquished control over a critical area of the business. I can remember thinking to myself, "You asked this guy to find a different way to sell your product. Just because it doesn't fit your personal fancy doesn't mean it's not right. Let the guy do his job."

So I turned Mark and his consultant Ric loose. They hired three telesales people and set up shop across the street in a temporary space, since they needed a quiet place to man the phones.

The plan was fairly simple. We would call golf pro shops from a nationwide list we had. We figured they were in the service business, and if this club helped their members it would be win/win: sales and service for us and a profit for them. We would say that we'd developed an exciting new golf club and that we'd like to send them a couple to try themselves and have their members hit.

Like all such ventures, we got some positive results and some outright refusals. Even when we did ship, some follow-up calls revealed that the box had never been opened. This was not unusual given that we were forcing ourselves into the game, but with time and repeat calls we started to get some positive responses. This was the beginning of 1996; in 1995 our sales had reached the $1 million level for the first time. Almost all of that was custom clubs, though. I had never dreamed of $1 million in sales. It's not that I thought it was impossible, I just didn't think in terms of volume. One might say that, given our performance over the years, that was a helpful defense mechanism and I'd probably agree. All I knew was that we had reached the $1-million mark.

Not all decisions were made without "discussion." I remember an early lunch meeting with Mark and Ric in which they told me their plan included selling the Tight Lies for $129 retail. As I choked on my food I asked them why, with competitive clubs priced at $199 and higher, they picked $129. Their answer reminded me of all the excuses I'd heard over the years. No one knows us. No one on tour uses the club. The same old rigmarole. I said something to the effect of, "No way. The price will be $199, end of discussion. At $129 I don't need salespeople. This is a great product and $199 is a fair price." Sometimes the pure entrepreneur in me surfaces. It was my butt on the line, my name, and my decision. The price was $199, and it was never a problem.

Letting Go and Establishing a Culture

As your company grows, you will inevitably have to let go of control over certain areas of your business. Some areas are easy to let go of like, for me, accounting. Once Adams Golf started growing I knew I had to get help in this area because I did not have the skills to do it myself. In sales, however, I knew I could sell. I had plenty of sales experience, and turning that over was traumatic for me.

This is one of the most difficult things you'll encounter. You didn't start up and spend endless days and nights on the business so you could say to someone, "Okay, all yours now." You may be thinking that you could plug someone into a position of authority but remain in charge, and to a degree you'd be right. Yes, you'd still be in charge and I guarantee you'd see things that you could do better. You can drop the occasional hint or schedule sit-down sessions, but if you start telling the people you hire how to do their jobs you'll be developing managers who will come to resent you.

Ceding control is relatively easy for an outside advisor, especially if he has never been an entrepreneur, but your soul, your persona, does not walk away from significant tasks easily. I wish I had some foolproof formula to give you, but I don't. In my case I was the personnel department, advisory staff, and janitor, all in one. This is the reality of a start-up, and the best I have to offer is recognition. This *will* happen. You won't necessarily like it, but that's how you'll grow. Just be clear with your objectives, always be honest, communicate, and trust your instincts.

The one thing you can and should do is to establish the culture. How do you want your company to be known? For example, I had a thing about housekeeping. I couldn't stand the idea of working all those years, finally getting into a nice building, and having people treat it shabbily. This included the office and the production area, and if I thought the mess had exceeded my limit I would come in late at night with my trusty camera and take pictures. The next day these would be publicly displayed with cryptic comments by the "midnight photographer" and the message was delivered. But you can't have high standards in one area and ignore others. To me, housekeeping was like customer service—a matter of product quality. And the same level of standards applies across the board. How do you motivate employees to work at a high level when the restrooms are a mess? You'll never know unless you inspect.

I see businesses that have reserved parking next to the door for the "big dogs," but this is something we never did at Adams Golf. My policy was that if you wanted a good spot, you had to get to work early. It's a pretty simple policy that drives home the point that we're all in this together. On the other hand I've seen plenty of places where the culture dictated very long hours because that's what the boss did and it was "expected." What baloney. Who are you to dictate that someone be away from their family and outside life just to keep up some kind of phony criteria? This is a power trip, plain and simple. "Better do like me if you want to succeed. After all, I'm the big dog with all the juice. Just look at my parking place."

Remember, we're talking about winning the game, and that includes building a positive work environment. One of the greatest stories I've ever heard is about the supermarket industry, specifically Publix stores. Founded by one of my favorite people, George Jenkins, Publix had such a good culture in the late 1970s when I knew them that, if an employee left, the competitors would be reluctant to hire them. Publix was such a good place to work that good people wouldn't leave. That was the kind of culture I wanted for Adams Golf, and while I couldn't "meddle," I could be the keeper of that flame.

Since I'm doing the writing, it's only fair that I go to great lengths to point out that I was no picnic to work for, no source of sweetness and light flitting around making sure everyone was happy. Neither is this an apology, as I have not softened with age. I did what I thought was best, and to the best of my ability enforced the highest standards. I slept okay then and still do now.

NINETEEN

THE MARKETING CHALLENGE

The telesales program started working, and the Tight Lies club picked up a certain degree of popularity in 1996. In fact, our sales closed at $3 million that year, a 300 percent increase, due to the telesales and our custom-fitting efforts. While we were happy, with the growth more issues arose. I had enough experience, both in golf marketing and with ball flight on the range, to know we had a good thing; the question was what to do with it.

Frankly I would have been happy with the growth if I hadn't spoken to a customer. He said, "Barney, I love the Tight Lies, but I'm sending back my inventory of twelve pieces. I use it myself, but in this business you have to get people coming to my store asking for the club. You don't do that, and unless you do you're going to lose any chance of this club selling." It was like a mini-industry survey, and he wasn't mincing words.

There is a great deal of marketing in golf, but true innovation is rare, and with the Tight Lies I was getting my chance (probably my only chance) at a piece of the proverbial pie. I didn't know or care where the Tight Lies would rank as an all-time great club; all I knew was that it had a chance to succeed.

There were a few other factors that I had to stop and consider. I was fifty-seven, had no money, no savings, and was pretty much unemployable having been on my own for so long. Our sales had actually produced a small bank account and I had retired—actually, burned—my credit card collection. We were generating enough to keep the company alive, yet nothing close to growth capital. Personally I was in less debt, but still far from secure in my financial future. Adams Golf had come a long way, yet the best description was that it was still a hand-to-mouth operation.

My only backup plan was teaching golf. I had spent thousands of hours on the range as a club-fitter, had the opportunity to observe several acclaimed teachers, and had picked their brains about their teaching influences, both in person and in written text. It wasn't hard to combine simple lessons with some of my club-fitting, so I had a semblance of a plan. Of course, it was missing a few things like health insurance and retirement, but if I was lucky I could stay off food stamps.

I'm being a bit lighthearted about this, but what I clearly remember is not daring to think about failure. Even though I was unemployable and in debt, I was now actually thinking about success. My passion was still there, and for the first time a glimmer of success appeared on the horizon.

It's fair to say that I was aware of the situation—after ten-plus years of failure there was finally a light at the end of the tunnel. Whether the light represented ultimate success or an oncoming train was yet to be determined but, in January of 1996, we went to the PGA show in Orlando with our new telesales group, a measured optimism, and a slightly bigger booth than usual. I had attended the show for years, at first by myself and then with Max. It was always the same: poor location, people ignoring you as they walked by, and an overwhelming feeling of inferiority to the major brands.

I can remember setting up the booth the day before the show, and as I walked out of the show area I passed through the booths of the big companies. They dwarfed mine, and I felt physically smaller. How could I possibly compete? At previous shows I was there as a club-fitter, never really encroaching on their marketing turf. This was our first year selling the Tight Lies, and as I navigated their booths I admit I felt intimidated.

I decided to stop and have a conversation with myself before leaving the room. "Quit this self-pity routine," I said. "Your job isn't to whine about the bigger guys and how no one stops in your booth. Your goal is to do such a good job the people who attend the show will want to see what you have." And there on the convention floor I realized that what I was feeling was just another form of the WOW factor. Booth size and company size weren't the real issues. It was about delivering the message, getting show customers to say, "WOW, that's a great product." After all, they were golfers, and I'd already had the experience. This may sound a little strange, a guy standing in the aisle talking to himself, and all the more if anyone heard the conversation, but I remember it to this day and it worked. My attitude changed.

I'd had the same PGA Show booth neighbor for years, a company called Prize Possessions, which sold high-quality tournament prizes. The keys to this company were the two ladies who owned and ran the place, Sarah Foehl and Ginny Durfee, two of the nicest and classiest people I've ever met. While pleasant and friendly to everyone who visited, they also knew how to write orders and didn't miss an opportunity. I would hang out on the edge of their booth and try to snag some of the buyers who were leaving, figuring that if they just had a pleasant buying experience they might be open to another. I used to vacuum their booth when I did mine just to be sure I was on their good side.

When we went in 1996 it was still way early in the game, but I noticed a slight shift in the atmosphere. We had come up a notch. Upon returning to our facility, the sales performance of the Tight Lies was changing the game. As I now recognize it, though, our geographically scattered sales were really a solid market test, exactly what a real consumer products company does with a new product. But considering that our gross sales were $300,000 in 1994, $1 million in '95, and would be $3 million in '96, I would have laughed away market test talk. So on the one hand sales were good, but they also served as a constant reminder that we needed some way to market our innovation.

But then I received some inspiration in the form of Lee Trevino, whose son, Tony, worked with me at the Haney Golf Ranch. When Tony saw and hit the Tight Lies he said, "You've got to make one for my dad. He'll love it." I was not going to turn down a chance to get a club to Lee Trevino, so I gladly complied. It wasn't long after that when I got a call at home. The voice on the other end of the line said, "Barney, this is Lee Trevino. That's the best fairway wood I've ever hit. Do you mind if I take it to Spalding next week? If I convince them to market it, you better get a good agent to negotiate a deal."

Just getting a call at home from one of the greatest golfers of this generation made my day (and month), and I of course told Lee to have at it. He was good to his word, but Spalding wasn't interested. The incident got me thinking about other possible partners, so I started to consider other companies that would be a good fit.

My next target was Wilson. I had enough contacts there to arrange a test in Dallas. They agreed to send someone down, and I would take him to the Haney Ranch. When the day came I met a nice young man who in answer to my questions told me he was an MBA from a very fine school. The idea was for him to try the club personally and listen to my plan of how it would fit into the Wilson structure.

We drove to the ranch and I picked up my sample Tight Lies and a bucket of practice balls. My friend from Wilson reached immediately for a Tight Lies to hit, which was a giveaway, as he had used no warm-up period. I figured he was young, obviously strong, and what the heck, it's us old guys who need a warm-up. His first shot wasn't exactly a shot. In fact, there was very little contact. The second shot almost decapitated the guy twenty-five feet down the line and at a 90-degree angle, so I suggested we might want to conduct a private test at the back of the range. I didn't know what my insurance liability was, but I knew I needed to be in a less populated area.

We jumped in a cart, and on the way over he told me that he was really a tennis player, had worked that side for Wilson, and had just recently been transferred to golf. He also admitted that he was new to playing the game. No kidding. At the back of the range, I started by giving him a few general tips on the golf swing, and while he generated terrific club head speed, making solid contact was his issue. About ten attempts into the session, the stars aligned for him (and me) and he hit a beautiful high draw at least 235 yards in the air. I immediately took the club from his hands and announced that the test was over. When he asked why, I said, "If that shot you just hit doesn't convince you of what this club can do, nothing will." Then I went on to explain to him how I saw the Tight Lies fitting into Wilson.

After we discussed options, he left, telling me that I'd be hearing from them relatively soon. I'm still waiting. Truly, I think he saw the merit in the Tight Lies but corporate experts at Wilson must've disagreed. Disappointed but unbowed, I prepared for my next presentation and the one I really wanted: Arnold Palmer Golf.

Arnie had been my golf hero ever since I saw him in Pennsylvania in the 1960s. With all due respect to Jack Nicklaus, Arnie was my man. He'd had his name on a golf company for many years with some success, but none recently. Here was my chance. I would come riding into Palmer Golf, save the day with my Tight Lies, and with tears of gratitude Arnie would invite me to be his partner in his Member Guest Tournament at Augusta. Fantasy aside, I knew the Tight Lies was perfect for them, so I arranged testing with key people and prepared a business plan for a successful implementation.

The guy who was to be my entry hit the Tight Lies great. It couldn't have been a better demonstration, and he left promising to get back to me. He did, and the conversation went something like this: "Barney, we're going to pass on the Tight Lies. It's really a great club, but we have a new technology that's going to revolutionize the golf equipment industry, and we're putting all our resources behind it." Disappointed but naturally curious, I said, "I understand. Any chance you can give me a hint about this new technology?" He said, "It's going to be announced shortly. We're going to offer graphite-shafted irons with no grips. Instead, the top part, the butt of the shaft, will be enlarged. It will have fantastic feel and make for new standards in shot control."

Yours truly being a college graduate (remember, I had a scholarship), an experienced businessman, and an overall good citizen, I erupted into the phone, "You know, I have years on the range, and with all due respect, without exception that idea has no chance of success." (Actually, the wording was a bit more colorful. A lot more.) A silence ensued, followed by a polite, "Thank you for your opinion." The rest is history. I had further established my credentials of being able to cross the line from honest opinion to total jerk. Was I right? 100 percent. They made the move, and it was the straw that broke their company.

Going zero for three was a bit painful, especially the Palmer episode. I had one more shot at a major company, but encountered the same negative results and was now zero for four. I figured I had pretty much exhausted the normal approach and it was time to start thinking differently. I first tried the major golf magazines, coming up with a plan that included free advertising in return for a percentage of the sales. They thanked me for thinking of them and explained that such an approach would definitely curtail their ad sales efforts with any other golf company. So I had exhausted print media, failed at trying to find a corporate partner, and the clock continued to tick. Still, there were encouraging signs. We were selling well (by my standards) and getting letters of praise from consumers, but also letters from our distribution channel telling us that we needed to do something about increasing consumer demand.

I knew the product was good. The fact that it had been reviewed and found lacking by the executives and staff of four major golf companies just meant they were missing an opportunity. This is either the complete testimonial to the power of WOW, or I was in serious need of a long rest in a quiet place. We referred to the Tight Lies as our WOW product. Why couldn't the "experts" understand?

TWENTY

WHAT ABOUT AN (GULP) INFOMERCIAL?

I don't remember the exact first moment the idea of an infomercial was raised. A couple of years earlier, one of my customers had said something like, "Have you ever thought of an infomercial?" in reference to an earlier product, and since I had never seen one, I said no. It turned out that he was associated with a very successful health and fitness show, and I got a brief education on the results from his project. He had given me some names of key players in the industry, and in my memory bank was the experience selling the Pelz inventory on HSN, so I knew how powerful TV could be.

Over the years several people have reminded me that they were the ones who prompted me to do an infomercial, but I have no clear recollection of any specific conversation. It was endlessly discussed on and off, probably because my favorite thing to do was whine about the market not accepting our wonderful product.

The truth is that there were already infomercials for golf products at that time, and the ones I watched all shared a common theme: Say anything and promise anything, regardless of the so-called technology. I remember one infomercial for a training device in which a high handicapper used the device for a few days and showed remarkable improvement in his golf swing. I happened to know the guy, and he was a very good player going in. His challenge was to look bad! Another infomercial from this time featured a host of golfers extolling the praises of a "revolutionary" new club. Just by accident, I'm sure, the members of this same group were investors in the company, all of them.

Let's face it. I didn't have a truckload of options, so I started studying golf infomercials. I learned that the most successful shows were about fitness both physical and emotional, diet, and financial success. And the simple reason is money. Virtually everyone who watches TV understands they can improve themselves in one or more of those areas. This means that when you have a show on these subjects you can run it on any cable network at any time of day. Golf, on the other hand, concerns only about 5 percent of the TV watchers, so this type of show has to be advertised on specific cable outlets to be successful. You have to get enough viewers to call in and buy the product so you can reinvest that money in more airtime.

Suffice it to say that for a period of time in 1996 I became the world's foremost expert on golf infomercials—the good ones, the bad ones, and the ones that never made it past test. There were two that I considered good: Wally Armstrong's training aids for the golf swing, and the one for the Alien wedge. The Alien was current and it was hot. Starting from nothing, the company had found a unique golf club, recruited investors to fund their effort, and produced an infomercial. Within months their sales went nuts. They were moving thousands per month, and as I learned more I became fixated on the process.

For those of you who don't suffer from insomnia, let me explain in more detail how infomercials work. You produce a half-hour TV show that extols your product, shows remarkable results, and is designed to get viewers reaching for the phone. To influence this action not only is the product available, but calls made within a certain amount of time also get a variety of add-ons or supplementary products for free. You are required by law to offer a money-back guarantee, which I assume is an attempt to regulate some of the, *ahem*, promises made. The makers of these shows are smart. They make the money-back offer sound as if they were offering their firstborn, and if this sounds a bit like the booths at state fairs, it isn't far removed. In fact, some of the folks I met in the industry had that exact background.

I'm not biting the hand that worked for us—I'm setting the stage. Some very large and successful companies have used this medium. It is an entrepreneur's dream, and I became excited about the prospect. The process is to produce a show and test it in a variety of markets. The result is one of the things I love most about infomercials: You know your return immediately.

Let's say you produce a show for a magic face cream. It's a new product, and you have a price point but are flexible, with sales being the objective. In other words, you can meet your margin goals at a price of say, ten dollars, but sometimes thirteen will actually sell better. A show, while a half-hour long, is really three shows of ten minutes each, and at the end of each segment is the "call to action." There are two main reasons for this approach. One is that you don't need a half-hour to tell your story. These products are what I call "see-wants." You see it, get a quick story and, under the blanket of the money-back guarantee, you want it. The other reason is logistical. You can't advertise an infomercial—the guide says, "paid programming." People who watch are clickers passing through the channels. The odds of them clicking through at the beginning of the infomercial are slim, and even if they do, they likely won't watch the entire show. That's why you see the use of well-recognized faces or very attractive folks, all designed to make you stop clicking, watch a bit, and buy. It also means the group that produces the show must have the expertise to deliver a quick, easily digestible message in each segment.

Using my face cream example, you can design a variety of requests to buy. You can also try a couple of price points, or make whatever variations you want to the test process. Next, you work with an operation that specializes in buying airtime, ideally one with not only a good track record but also experience in your product line. Infomercials are a product of cable. Networks don't run them, but with the proliferation of cable and satellite dishes, we now have eight jillion channels that need something to show in the off hours. During the test period you try as much variety as you can afford, and a relatively few showings give the airtime buyers enough data to know if your show will be a success, which version, at what price point, and where and when to run it. You do not field the calls; that task gets contracted out to a call center that handles several shows simultaneously. The reason for that is logistics. You need people on the phones 24/7 since, when people call, it's the only chance you'll get to sell. Of course, one show doesn't run that often, so each phone at the call center has forty-two lines, and the operator knows which numbers are yours. This precludes answering the face cream inquiry with a fertility drug sales pitch. Some successful shows have dedicated operators. Again, this is big business and only the good survive.

Even the process of shipping is handled elsewhere. Each order comes with a credit card number. The card must be processed and shipping labels produced, and specialty software and a variety of products are needed to accomplish that. Tens of thousands of people are employed in the infomercial business, which includes a great deal of sophistication that belies what is seen on some of the shows.

All of that expertise, refined over many years, allows you to accurately predict the revenues your show will produce. This is critical for buying initial inventories and preparing your company for the short-term results. There is an old adage in traditional advertising: "I know fifty cents of every dollar is wasted, I just don't know which fifty cents it is." An infomercial is not for everyone, but in the right environment it's a perfect advertising expense. You can track your specific return weekly.

Armed with this knowledge I went in search of a partner, and approached two established infomercial companies. These were businesses that, if they liked your product, would produce the show, buy the airtime, and essentially become your partner. I remember clearly that both companies were pretty similar in their approach. It started with keeping me waiting for a very long time when I arrived for the meeting. Then they told me of the great risks involved and the statistics of how many shows produced actually make it through test. The spiel segued into what a tough business it was, and how even with their great expertise they had to fight the good fight daily.

They both offered me a deal, each incredibly lopsided arrangements in which they would receive almost all of the profits and I would only see money way, way down the line if the show became a colossal hit.

I understood that the guy who puts up the money calls the shots, and that is completely fair. It just didn't work for me. I wasn't a guy with an idea trying to make a few bucks. I was trying to find a way to get the marketing support I needed to build my company.

So my great idea turned a bit sour. It didn't mean the idea of an infomercial was wrong; it just presented a larger challenge. We'd have to find a way to fund the project internally, and also to handle critical logistics ourselves. I called a administrative staff meeting, our staff at the time being me, Ann Neff, and Patty Walsh. I'm pleased to say as I write this that Ann and Patty still work at Adams, and now have titles and offices. Back then they had neither, and without their talents and willingness to suffer my manic pace, Adams Golf would be long gone by now. I convinced them that internally handling the necessary logistics was something they could do in addition to their already overwhelming workloads, and started the process of raising the necessary funds.

My presentation to my investors was more like a plea. Sure, I went the whole nine yards with charts, profit projections, customer references; it was a very polished approach. But no matter how well I presented this approach it came with the odor of desperation, which is not conducive to people reaching for their checkbooks. Furthermore, our (okay, *my*) track record over the past years hadn't been inspirational, which meant that I wasn't dealing from a position of strength.

Essentially, my presentation boiled down to this: "You know this company is all I have. It's taken my every effort over these last ten years to achieve a few minor victories. As I stand here I'm fifty-seven years old without a dime to my name. Whatever its value, this company represents everything I have, both financially and emotionally. Our sales are approaching $3 million in 1996, and with any modest growth I can make a livable wage from the company. However, for investors there isn't much chance for a good payback. We have a unique opportunity with the Tight Lies, though, and I'm convinced with proper marketing it has great potential.

"I need a commitment for approximately $700,000 to internally fund an infomercial. This pays for the production of the show, test marketing, and a percentage for buying inventory and contingencies. I do not have any money to contribute, so I will give you the only asset I have—Adams Golf. Let me be clear: I will pledge all of my ownership in the company against your investment. I have prepared an earn-out schedule based on sales and profits far in excess of anything the company has ever accomplished so, if successful, I can earn back my equity and you will be glad to give it to me."

Know what they said? WOW. And they agreed to support my plan. Did it happen exactly like that? No, but pretty close. It was obviously a bit more complicated, but at the end of the day I got the money and we made the equity deal. Was it my faith, my willingness to put it all on the line that influenced their decision? Who knows? There was no elaborate contract. In fact, there was no legal agreement of any kind. I presented my case, they agreed, and we shook hands. It turned out to be a multimillion dollar agreement, and there was never any question about our mutual intentions.

I've been told that I really wasn't risking much, that in truth the company wasn't that valuable, and I have one answer to that: absolutely no way. We were at $3 million in sales even without successful marketing at that time, with a good window to more than $5 million, and coming from where I started that was a very successful level—one from which I could personally make a decent living. Further, the psychological impact of my offer weighed very heavily over the coming months. Very, very heavily.

Barney and the original
Tight Lies at the Haney
Ranch

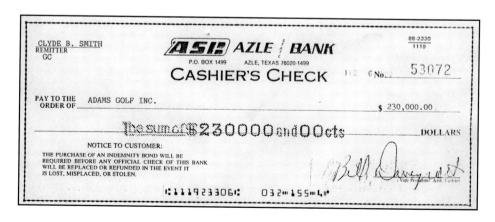

The "miracle" check from Clyde Smith

Hank Haney with an early Adams putter

Full fitting cart at the Haney Ranch, including the Distance Caddy, a radar for accurately measuring shot distance

Max Puglielli fits a senior golfer at the Haney Ranch.

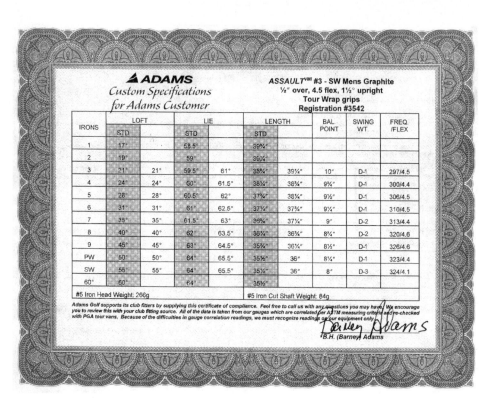

Every custom-fit customer received a certificate—a WOW service.

2,500 square foot manufacturing facility, 1994

Indoor fitting and data collection at Adams using very sophisticated computer monitoring

1996 PGA staff

(From left to right) Carol Mann, LPGA and World Golf Hall of Fame; Jack Whitaker, Emmy Award winner and member of the American Sportscasters Hall of Fame; Hank Haney, 1993 PGA Teacher of the Year; Barnyard; Bill Rogers, 1981 PGA Player of the Year and British Open Champion.

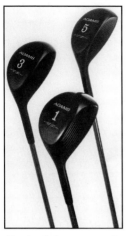

Early Adams woods

Early Adams irons

MacClain Sand Wedge (concave face), 1928

Original Farlie anti-shank wedge, 1891

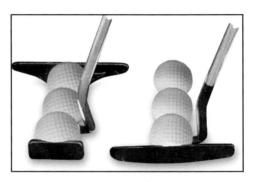

Pelz 3 ball putters

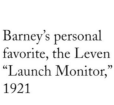

Modern Anti-Shank Wedge

Barney's personal favorite, the Leven "Launch Monitor," 1921

Troon club

Horton multiple
material wood

Weir offset wood,
1905

Currie metal
wood, 1891

Slade spring face wood,
1896

Kent adjustable weight wood, 1917

Hutchinson
square driver,
1892

Tooley perimeter weighted iron, 1905

Approximately half the clubs used on the road, 1993

Not par for the course

Golf manufacturer gets club in hands of players with unconventional methods

Barney Adams should feel triumphant, and part of him does.

The founder of Adams Golf Inc. has just returned from the biggest trade show of the year with more than $500,000 in golf club orders in his pocket.

He sold more in just 3½ days at the PGA Merchandise Show in Orlando, Fla., than his tiny Plano company unloaded in all of 1994.

His patented Tight Lies fairway wood — proclaimed golf's breakthrough product of 1996 by a leading industry group — is all the talk on professional tours, with such names as Tom Watson, Jack Nicklaus and Jan Stephenson giving them a swing.

When Gibby Gilbert won last Sunday on the Senior PGA Tour, two Tight Lies were in his bag, and Mr. Adams didn't pay an endorsement fee to get them there.

Three golf-equipment giants recently hit him up about selling out. A year and a half ago, he'd have crawled on all fours to land such suitors. Today, he's told them to go jump.

"It's hard to describe the phenomenon compared to where we were 15 months ago, which was nowhere," he says, leaning back in his chair at

Please see TINY on Page 12H.

CHERYL HALL
IDEAS AT WORK

The Dallas Morning News: Juan Garcia

Barney Adams, founder of Adams Golf Inc., says, "We are by no means — by no means — a major player in this business, but we're starting to build a little niche with an excellent reputation."

The Cheryl Hall story that earned national attention for Adams, 1997

Send comments and tips through e-mail to:
sports@tampatrib.com
MIKE PENNETTI, Golf Editor (813) 259-7893
Sports fax, (813) 259-8148

GOLFEXTRA

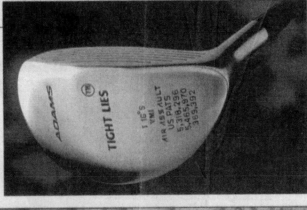

Tight Lies
and truth in
advertising
turn Adams
Golf Co. into
an unlikely
success story
— with a cult
following.

**Adams Golf's line
of Tight Lies
fairway woods
helped give
Barney Adams'
company more
than $35 million
in sales last year,
nearly 12 times
its previous best.**

Tight Lies story in *The Tampa Tribune*, 1998

Barney with spokesman
Tom Watson

Nick Faldo at Chelsea Pier during the road show, 1998

CEO Chip Brewer with Tom Watson

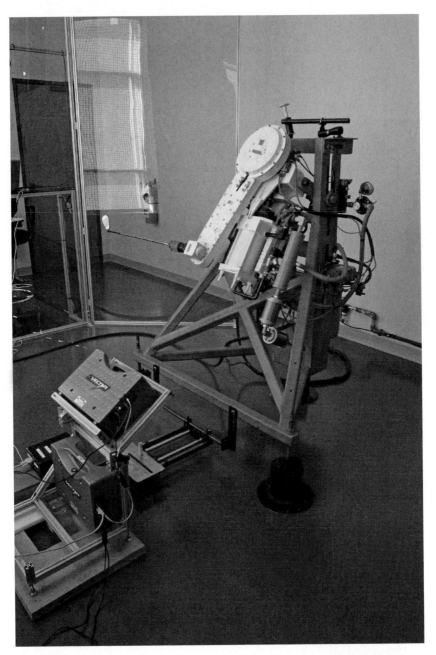

Indoor testing at Adams Golf using the Iron Byron, originally designed by Bob Bush at True Temper Sports, Inc. after
the swing of Byron Nelson

Barnyard deep in thought after a long day making a commercial

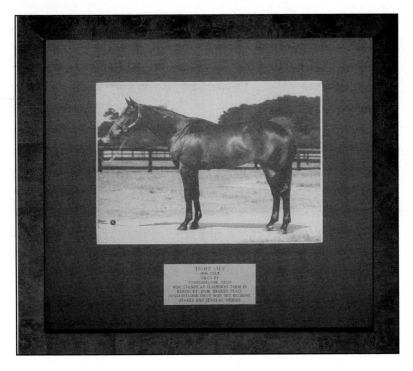

A happy customer named his prize-winning racehorse Tight Lies

Adams Golf Headquarters, Plano, Texas

TWENTY-ONE

STARTING THE INFOMERCIAL PROCESS

*N*ow that I had funding, I started looking at independent infomercial production companies and found that I could get a show made for production costs ranging from $125,000 to $500,000. Naturally, the $125,000 guy told me his work was as good as his more expensive competitors, just more efficient, so I sought out the advice of someone with experience. I managed to get the name of the architect of the successful Alien Wedge show, Jim Harrison, and he told me to contact a production company in Santa Ana, California, called Script to Screen. In Jim's words they were "not the cheapest, but the best."

If you believe in omens, I encountered one immediately. The financial backer of Script to Screen was a man by the name of Bill Mitchell, who happened to be a very good golfer and was playing a Tight Lies. His first comment to me was, "I've been looking for you. This is a great club, and I immediately thought it would be a great infomercial." I soon met the staff. Tony Kerry handled the sales and business side, while his brother Ken took care of the creative end. In our first meeting I outlined my thoughts for the show, the fact that they had experience and I didn't notwithstanding. And though I wasn't an expert when it came to infomercials, I did have a vision for the show that was just as strong as my premonition about Haney or the design of the Tight Lies.

After the business part was settled we began the process of creating the show. I'm sure they assumed that was their role. Little did they know what kind of nutcase they were dealing with. My first premise was nonnegotiable: Everyone who appeared on the show would be a real customer. We would use real stories and real golf shots. They were very polite and said something like, "Ah, Barney, you do remember this is an infomercial." And in response I said something to the effect that selling was okay, but if it meant breaking new ground, that was old hat for me. I had created my small company by custom-fitting clubs and improving ball flight, and that attitude—that search for the truth—would be part of the show. Suffice it to say, it's a testament to their good nature that they suffered me in the ensuing months.

Ken and his staff visited Dallas and we conducted a ball-hitting session so they could get a feel for the features and benefits of the Tight Lies. They talked to me about "talent," and explained the need for someone with stopping power; we discussed several names for the host and narrator, with our first choice being Jack Whittaker. I was a fan and delighted when we were able to sign him up. After Jack, we used people who had significant experience with the club: Hank Haney; former PGA player-of-the-year Bill Rogers; and LPGA Hall-of-Famer Carol Mann. Supplementing them were several other teaching pros and amateur users.

Ken Kerry was in charge of the script and the concept for the show, and I became his royal pain. It's no exaggeration to say that I reviewed every word. When we got the first videos, I would go over every minute, often long into the night, leaving Ken phone messages at 3:00, 4:00, 5:00 A.M. I don't know if I helped. After all, Ken was a successful professional. I understood he would do his best to produce a functional show. I was merely struggling with a life-and-death mentality. When we finished the show, the Kerrys were very pleased with the results. It was time to test the market.

I also had to learn what our show's objective was. Of course, it was to sell product, but it was more complex than that. Some shows have strictly that goal: sell product, make as much money as you can. Our objective was different, because we wanted to use the show to build distribution within the golf industry.

Say, hypothetically, that you buy a half-hour on the Golf Channel or a regional sports network and, for the sake of argument, let's say the airtime costs $1,000. When the show is played, you get sales of $6,000. Figuring in product and handling costs of an additional $1,000, you get a return of 3:1. (This is clearly an exceptional performance, but I'm using easy numbers.)

If you're in the deal to make money you take out as much as you can, leaving only enough to buy another half-hour. The data shows (or did then) that less than 10 percent of the interested parties who watch an infomercial actually pick up the phone, but many others will look for the product at retail. Our goal was to build a company with retail distribution (retail being golf specialty stores and golf pro shops), so in my example we would reinvest the entire $6,000 to buy more exposure on television.

This is an example of the decisions involved in a successful show. At the time I had no idea if we would sell anything. All of our previous efforts at mass marketing had failed, and experienced companies had turned us down. Yet I was convinced it was a matter of the medium and the message. And the first step was to test our show in a variety of markets.

About a month beforehand I started experiencing nightmares. Whatever the situation, whether it involved guns, knives, or cliffs, there was one common theme: I lost. I'd wake up in a cold sweat, short of breath. It didn't take a psychologist to figure out what was causing my trauma. As the test period got closer the nightmares increased in frequency and intensity.

I tried my best not to involve myself in the thought process of figuring out what would happen if the infomercial failed, at least not until immediately prior to the test period. But one night I was sitting in my office late and tried to engage in a bout of reality. What do I do if this is a bust? I asked myself. It wasn't as if everyone I knew was telling me not to worry. In fact, to the best of my recollection it was pretty much the opposite. That evening reality became overwhelming. If this failed, I was done for good. I would lose my company. And at age fifty-seven, without a penny to my name, the prospect of failure was traumatic—even more so than in the past— because this time there was a victory that could be identified.

As we were starting the test period, I went on a sales trip with our representative from North Carolina. Frankly, the trip wasn't critical but I had to get away. Everything was out of my hands and I needed a diversion. We were to get first returns at a specific time, and I was to call in. As the time approached we were somewhere on the border of North Carolina and Georgia, in an area so remote that cell phones didn't get reception. We came upon a rest stop and I ran from the car to the pay phone. When I returned to the car the rep noticed my manner and said, "Must have been good news." "Nope," I said. "In fact there was no news at all. The phone was out of order. But out of habit I checked the return coin slot, and lying there was $4.80 in coins. I'm not much of a believer in signs, but this is the real deal. We're going to be fine." I had no more knowledge than I've just described, but when I found all that change, a feeling came over me that I cannot explain. I just knew we were going to succeed.

The Tight Lies infomercial went on to be the highest-grossing golf club infomercial in TV history. Since then, many years have passed and I doubt if it still holds that status. It transformed our business, changed my life, changed the life of Script to Screen, and in several ways it changed the golf industry. Obviously, on the way to Georgia I wasn't privy to any of this knowledge. I was just quiet and happy, two descriptions rarely used about me. When I got to the Motel 6 it was too late to call in, so the next morning I got the report. Infomercials are described in baseball language, from singles to home runs, and with some success and some failures we were considered a double. We generated enough sales to keep the show on the air and that was a good start. When I got home I looked at the results in detail and found one strange omission: we had bought no time on the Golf Channel. And since we were dealing with the buying group directly, I called and talked to the person buying our TV time.

Sometimes in business you encounter a person, however capable, who is in a different zone or space than you and that was the case when I called. After asking some questions about the TV channels used I asked why not the Golf Channel. I didn't pretend any great expertise, but asked, "This is a golf club; they are the Golf Channel. Why did we skip them and go on the Sewing Channel?" A decipherable answer was never forthcoming, and they continued to ignore the Golf Channel. So I found another time buyer, and the first thing they asked me was, "Why aren't you on the Golf Channel?"

Soon we were, and the results amazed everyone.

TWENTY-TWO

THINGS START TO CHANGE

*T*he story I've written up to this point has been one of hanging on in the face of continued failure. The great golfer of the 1930s, Bobby Jones, has been quoted as saying that he learned more from losing a tournament than he ever did from winning one. At the rate he won, I'll assume the lessons were from early failures. We certainly had plenty of those, but it was time to start experiencing some extraordinarily good results.

Our first taste of success came in late 1996 when we first tested the infomercial and got a bit of a sales increase and momentum heading into the 1997 PGA Merchandise Show. With our infomercial in its test period, our goal was to increase retail sales. We wanted people who saw the show to go to retailers and ask for the product. Golf equipment is sold primarily in retail golf specialty stores as opposed to on-course shops, the ratio being roughly 88 percent off-course to 12 percent on-course. We effectively had no off-course distribution at this time and no outside sales force, so our plan was to use the show to create product awareness. As consumers sought the product at retail we would be following up with our customers via telephone.

Two other things happened. We moved from my little shop to a cavernous building of some 25,000 square feet, necessary to accommodate our growing staff. The distance was only a couple of miles, but psychologically the decision was overwhelming. We also increased our booth space at the 1997 PGA show.

It's hard to describe the effect of the national PGA show as it was in those days. If a small company like Adams, which hung on with minimal space in the back of the building, suddenly moved to a better location with more space, something was going on. It could have just been an infusion of cash followed by an ego move, or it could have meant the company was becoming more popular. In our case it was the latter. The WOW factor was starting to take effect.

We made another good decision in that same general time period. Outside of the infomercial we didn't have any money to advertise, but we knew we had a story and wanted to get the word out, this time to the golf media. Through a friend I became aware of an industry publicist by the name of Mary Beth Lacy, described to me as simply the best independent publicist in the business. When introduced we immediately clicked, and through her outstanding efforts getting us media exposure she became a vital part of our team.

The infomercial ran sporadically in early 1997 as we moved into golf season. Calling it a test period is relative. We had a limited amount of money to spend on airtime. Because of our retail growth strategy, every dime that came from show sales went back into more exposure, so whether you call it test or a rollout, it's the same thing.

As we continued to test the show, most retailers were responding to our phone sales efforts. We still had no field sales force, and one wasn't necessary. We were riding the buildup of a successful product, and for those of you who embrace the theory of focused marketing, that's exactly what we did. We weren't really in the golf equipment business. That would have meant drivers, fairway woods, irons, wedges, and putters. Yes, we made all those things as a holdover from our custom-fitting days but, as far as the market was concerned, we were in the fairway woods business only.

The show increased our visibility, so we added more telesales people and leveraged that visibility by bringing the entire sales operation in-house. A good field rep can make five calls a day, maybe thirty a week, and that's pushing it. But with telesales you can make thirty calls a day and, with a product growing in popularity like ours was, we didn't need clever displays or elaborate pitches. It was simply a matter of calling up customers and hearing them ask, "When can we get some?"

The Golf Channel was just getting started then, and like any new broadcast outlet they did not have a full schedule of material. We bought time. Our half-hour show worked, meaning we sold enough clubs to cover our costs and make a small profit. We increased our showings, and it was perfect. Any time we showed on the Golf Channel, it was successful. At one juncture we might have been their biggest advertiser, or close to it. The Golf Channel is still in business and they still occasionally run infomercials, but it's a different landscape now. A half-hour show costs a lot more now than it did back in 1997, and while it's true that they have many more viewers, it's still harder to keep a show on the air. But back then the stars aligned for us. The Golf Channel was critical to our success and they were glad to have our business.

During 1997 our plan never changed. We continued to reinvest because we wanted our show to be seen everywhere. There was also a secondary fact that drove us. Lots of infomercials sell product, but it's the returns that kill them. As I explained in an earlier chapter, every infomercial must, by law, offer a money-back guarantee. Our returns were virtually nil, and that fact was a sure sign that we were doing the right thing.

Our show increased exposure for us in 1997, and along the way we caught a couple of breaks. First, Lee Trevino took his Tight Lies with him to a Senior Tour event in New Jersey. Lee had already gone to bat for us at Spalding, but the fact that they declined a formal relationship did not diminish his enthusiasm. Lee Trevino loves golf, and when he gets a club that he really likes, he shows it to everyone. I wasn't there, but he had the club at the practice range before the event and was essentially doing a one-man demonstration, showing the other pros how easy Tight Lies was to hit. A writer for *Golf World* magazine saw him and picked up the story, reporting, "Trevino likes the club so much he may buy the company," a takeoff on the Remington razor story from a few years before. Trevino obviously didn't buy the company, nor did his sponsor Spalding follow up, but we got the best kind of press in golf: a professional praising a product because it worked, not because he was paid. The story was good enough that it was picked up in other publications as well. The "official" comment from the president of Spalding was that they always encourage Lee to look for new ideas, and I could hear his teeth clenching in print.

In February 1997, a local columnist in the *Dallas Morning News* by the name of Cheryl Hall interviewed us for a story emphasizing our long struggle and unconventional thinking by using telesales and the new infomercial. Obviously, I knew the story was coming. What I didn't know is that it would be on the front page of the Sunday business section. I remember that Sunday, reading the paper and the tremendous feeling of pride. I didn't realize how highly regarded Cheryl was until I found that her story had been picked up by hundreds of publications across the United States. As she pointed out in the article, we certainly had not arrived but we were at least getting up to the plate, and I'll be eternally grateful to Cheryl Hall and Lee Trevino.

One day around that time I was invited to lunch and golf at Preston Trail Golf Club, one of the finest clubs in all of Texas. My host was a charter member by the name of Charles Summerall, and over lunch he proceeded to talk to me about joining the club, telling me that the timing was excellent.

My investor board had been encouraging me to join a club for a year, and while the company was doing better, we were still far from a big success. I lived two miles from Preston Trail and really did love the place, but couldn't justify spending the money membership in the club required. Sure, Adams Golf had a little money in the bank, but I didn't think it was right to tap the proverbial till. I was discussing my situation with a friend at lunch a few days later and once again it took an outsider to correct my vision. "How old are you?" he asked. And when I answered fifty-eight, he said, "What are you waiting for? By the time you meet your own standards, you'll be too old to play." Immediately I knew he was right, but I still had a problem with using company money on the membership and certainly had none of my own to spend on it.

But what I did have were credit cards. I hadn't destroyed them all, and one of the ones I kept had a check-writing feature. But instead of writing a check against my credit card to pay for the membership, I took a more calculated risk. I had a friend who had just taken over as CEO of a company, and I knew he wouldn't have done so unless he felt he would succeed. So I wrote a check and bought stock in his company on margin. His presence had a positive effect and the stock was recommended. It quickly went up, so I sold, paid the taxes, and joined the club. Why on earth would I do something like that? It was convoluted logic, but I figured I'd been down so long I was due for a break.

The day after Cheryl Hall's story in the *Morning News* was the annual Valentine's Day party at Preston Trail. It was my first function as a member, and when my wife and I arrived we found ourselves standing right behind Byron Nelson, who was one of the course designers. When Byron, gracious as always, turned and said, "Nice story, Barney," I knew I was in for a highlight evening. Sure enough, my new fellow members were very complimentary as I moved throughout the room. They were so welcoming that I wasn't even self-conscious about wearing my $79 suit, the one reserved for the PGA show that I had bought at one of those no-label places. This was my night. Moving from one room to another, though, I glanced in a full-length mirror and immediately convulsed with laughter. Turns out I had neglected one small detail getting dressed that night—my fly was unzipped!

What a great experience and what a great lesson. It was the perfect self-administered putdown to a phony sense of being. I've used that story many times over the years, and it's not only the perfect story about small business; it's a perfect story about life.

The year 1997 might have been the happiest in my golf career. We had forecast that sales might double, but with the good publicity and the building momentum we dared to think that we could reach $10 million, triple the sales of the previous year. The telesales group was growing and we started to fill the new facility. Then, at the '97 PGA show, we wrote orders for over $500,000 worth of Tight Lies, a figure that exceeded sales from all the other PGA shows I had attended combined. We were slowly opening new accounts and more importantly getting reorders as the club sold through quickly.

Golf is funny. People hear about a hot club and they want one immediately. One day Sean Connery called, and it took the girls in the office two days to settle down. Clint Eastwood stopped by our booth at a PGA Show, and they went nuts again. Professional athletes, celebrities, would call to get their Tight Lies. We were a question on Jeopardy, worked into TV Shows like "The King of Queens." From where we started, Adams Golf became an exciting place to come to work and the enthusiasm rubbed of on our employees.

The infomercial started to kick in as the year went on, and we were able to increase its presence on the air. Our sales approach worked perfectly, and instead of reaching the unheard of goal of $10 million in sales for the year, we hit that number by April. And by the end of the year we had reached $30 million. Believe it or not, even bigger things were in store for us in 1998.

TWENTY-THREE

FIRST HALF OF 1998, AMAZING

*W*e entered 1998 with all the momentum from our tenfold sales growth in 1997. Our formula worked beyond our wildest imagination and, while in '97 we still had some semblance of control, it's fair to say we lost it in 1998. First, sales shot up from $30 million to $85 million. We increased staff twentyfold, had to devise an infrastructure concurrent with our growth, and dealt with the dozens of Tight Lies copies and knock-offs that flooded the market. We also moved again, this time into a 100,000-square-foot space, went public, and developed new product lines. Then we were hit with a recession in the industry, and learned that our marketing system was perfect for a growing new product, yet equally imperfect for daily competition. Those are just a few of the highlights. Any one or two of those events in one year would have been traumatic, but having all and more happen was beyond rational thought. I'm not embellishing what happened to get your attention, folks, and these were just *some* of the major issues.

The first indicator that things had grown beyond our control was the 1998 PGA Merchandise Show. This time we increased our booth space again, moving up to what the show calls "Main Street," where the big companies dwell. I wish I could remember who came up with our show marketing idea, because it was priceless. As I mentioned before, we were not allowed to sell product at the show. Many of the show's customers squeeze in a round of golf (or five) during their stay in Orlando, though, and some wanted a Tight Lies to use. Rather than ship one, we said, "Come by the booth and pick one up."

Somehow, word got out that the Tight Lies was "available at a special show price." We, of course, had nothing to do with spreading that news, but the result was spectacular, and soon there was a line extending from our booth literally a hundred feet long. This wasn't a one-time occurrence, either. It lasted for the better part of the first two days of the show. Neighboring booths complained (rightly so) that our line blocked entrance to their displays and the show personnel asked us to stop the practice (right after they got theirs). We complied, but we had achieved our goal. Hundreds of people were walking the PGA show carrying a Tight Lies. We couldn't have designed a better marketing display. At the end of the first day I overheard one of our competitors saying, "If one more person comes into our booth carrying one of those Tight Lies I don't know what I'll do." But the best part was when his companion said, "You ever hit one? WOW, they are really good." And remember the $500,000 in orders we wrote the year before? We beat that the first morning!

After the show we returned to Texas with the immediate goal of obtaining more heads and shafts to assemble. Fortunately, our suppliers had attended the show so we were able to start conversations with them, as well as with new sources just to keep up. We told our supplier to multiply our monthly order by five and that we'd let them know when to slow down.

In February we moved into our new, significantly larger space. This was such a monumental decision that we actually consulted with an outsider for advice, and his recommendation was not to undergo a change of that magnitude at such a difficult time in our business. We figured the move was inevitable and were used to challenges, so for us it was a question of how, not if. The building we moved to was brand-new and had been laid out to our specifications. Although I was involved in negotiating the lease, I hadn't visited the new building until one day in the fall of 1997. The place was huge and it intimidated me. Scared me to death. I could not in my wildest dreams imagine Adams Golf in such a facility, and never went back there until the day we moved.

Dick Murtland had been responsible for moving a large staff into a new building in his previous position, and he worked out a plan. The salespeople and necessary support team went to the PGA show and were gone a week. During that period, Dick organized the move, and when we returned all we had to do was to move our personal offices into the new space. On a scale of one to ten the move would rate a twelve. Within two weeks it was like we'd been there forever. I couldn't resist bringing the expert back to show him what Dick had done, and he was overwhelmed. This job had WOW factor in spades.

Our sales success invited one of the nasty elements of the golf equipment business—knockoffs. Golf is called a gentleman's game, and properly played that is a correct description. The world of equipment sales is like any business, though. It's a street fight, and knockoffs are a prime example of how that end of the game is played. I was aware of the practice, but it didn't make the experience any less nasty.

Copies and knockoffs are different. A copy is an illegal club that looks exactly like yours down to the name, shape, color, and every minute detail. Often the source is the same foundry that makes your heads. This is a much more common manufacturing practice in Asia than it is here in the United States. You can have your heads made here to protect yourself, but it would make no difference. The copiers will just buy clubs, send them overseas, and copy them anyway. It takes a sophisticated operation to be able to track down shipments and identify operations that are not your customers, yet are selling what appear to be your clubs. The big companies do pretty well at this, having developed sophisticated systems over the years, but we didn't have a clue. I'll never know how much business we lost to copies, but knowledgeable friends who were experienced in the Asian retail market told me years later that it was in the hundreds of thousands of units, and that does not seem unreasonable.

Knockoffs are a different animal. These clubs are designed to look like yours and fool people, but under close examination they are slightly different. And those slight visual differences can mark the difference between a legal and an illegal product. At one time we counted twenty-two different clubs that were knockoffs of one form or another. Knockoffs are not illegal as long as they are not pure copies. In fact, there is an entire knockoff industry, complete with consumers and manufacturers—"Just like the real thing, only much cheaper."

Nastiness reared its ugly head in other forms, too. At the 1998 PGA show, a writer for a national golf magazine approached me and said he apologized, but that in the interest of journalistic accuracy he had to follow up on a story he had just been told. Apparently the CEO of a smaller, competing club manufacturer (with a knockoff of the Tight Lies) told him (and others) that I used to work there. Moreover, he said that I had stolen the design for the Tight Lies and produced it under my name. My response was immediate: "Go back, tell them you're writing the story, and ask for employment records, W-2 forms, cancelled checks, something that proves I worked there. Tell them you spoke to me and that this was my suggestion. After all, employment is easy to prove. Also tell them that you need the documents for your story, and that failure to produce them will seriously damage their credibility." The writer came back a bit later, smiled, and said, "I delivered your message. There will be no story." Months later I was quietly walking a retail golf store and overheard that company's sales rep repeating the same lie. Like I said, it's a gentleman's game for those that play, but it's not that way on the business end, and these things continued on throughout much of the '98 golf season. I can think of dozens of other incidents but the theme never changed; the competition didn't have our product, so instead they took to attacking me and my company.

We developed some 7,500 retail and pro shop accounts across the United States in 1998. We also did business all over the world, and because of the infomercial some customers just called in direct. The process of opening an account was not a simple task. While most of the prospective customers are good, reliable businesses, when you're dealing with that kind of volume not all will be trustworthy. To safeguard against this, credit applications and references became necessary, as well as a system to process orders. We did not have a computerized system at the time and there was no way one could be developed that quickly. It was hard enough just hiring people and teaching them a basic procedure.

We could have slowed down and tried to work at a pace we could manage. But our objective was to build retail customers for the future. We had a hot product, and telling customers to get in line was not going to be the start of a beautiful relationship. Our plan was to give everyone great service and to take advantage of the phenomenon.

Our overseas distribution then led to another awakening, as we received notification of lawsuits regarding illegal usage of the names Adams and Tight Lies in two countries, England and Japan. The way the patent process works is that you file in the United States, and if you wish to file outside the U.S., there are fees by country, some of which are quite substantial. We couldn't afford any more than the minimum when we filed, and the growth outside the U.S. happened so quickly that we hadn't completed that part of the process. There are predators who look for situations like ours, and file patent claims in an attempt to negotiate lucrative settlements for themselves.

Insofar as all of these problems stemmed from our rapid growth and popularity, they were a pain—but not all that serious when compared to some of the old troubles we'd had. In meetings, I'd say, "If you think this is bad, let me tell you..." So we continued along our escalating growth path and the Tight Lies story grew. The media in all forms, print, radio, television, picked up on our success and thereby attracted a new group to our door: Wall Street.

Starting in about March of '98, some half-dozen different brokerage houses called on us inquiring if we'd ever considered going public. In a way it was funny, because until the previous six to eight months, all I had ever considered was survival. Going public was never something I contemplated or really knew anything about. But once the subject came up, a whole new realm of possibility entered into Adams Golf. Certainly our investors saw it as a way to capitalize on their investment, and as a shareholder I'd be a liar if I didn't consider the personal financial potential for myself, as well as for those employees who held stock. But the biggest benefit, as I saw it, was the chance to fund the company for future growth without absorbing crippling debt. Interest payments had sunk more than one company in the golf equipment industry, and all the brokerage houses told us of the spectacular success at Callaway after their public offering. We certainly knew we weren't Callaway, but the chance to have secure funding after all the years of living hand-to- mouth was the clincher. We decided to go public.

After all the romance, we picked Lehman Brothers, primarily because they had taken Cobra Golf public and we would be working with the same experienced team. After we made the choice, then the process began to see if we could really qualify as a public company. We knew next-to-nothing about the process, so we made the decision to give the attorneys and bankers every detail about our business. We essentially said if they did all the investigation, all the diligence, and came to the conclusion that we had a shot at going public, we'd agree. We wouldn't attempt to influence the decision or the stock price.

The process started in March of 1998 and our road show (which I'll explain below) was to begin in June. Sometime in May I got a call from Lehman suggesting that we postpone the offering until the fall. They felt we were approaching the vacation period and there was concern about being effective during the road show. I was visiting my friend Jim Marshall, whom I've described in the dedication of this book, when I returned the Lehman call. Their request sounded logical and I agreed over the phone that we'd set a later date. Since I was in Jim's living room at the time he got the essence of the conversation, and what followed was almost a repeat of the one-sided conversation I'd had with Rocky Thompson about the name Tight Lies back in 1995. Jim said, "Do I understand that you have the possibility to go public next month, and now you are agreeing to postpone for two or three months? That is purely stupid. Events out of your control could occur between now and then, and you might never get the chance. You have an opportunity, so take it now."

I always listened to Jim. Sometimes I'd offer an argument, but this time I said nary a word. Immediately I picked up the phone, called Lehman, and said I'd changed my mind. If we were going public, June was the date.

I returned to Texas and began preparations for the road show. Here we were in the middle of a sales boom, barely able to keep up, and it was time to take our top people on a three-week blitz. I've since had the opportunity to talk to others who participated in road shows prior to a public offering. It's a grueling pace. You make four to six presentations a day to representatives from potential investment companies. Your audience is experienced, and because they hear so many presentations they've got computer programs into which they plug your numbers to determine whether or not your company fits their parameters. We started in New York and three weeks later ended in Milan, Italy, having made more than sixty presentations.

Most of the people I've spoken with did not care for the process, or at least would not want to try it again. Personally, I loved it. I have no idea why, but it was like some monster challenge. If life was a blur before, this process was a blur at high speed. But I do remember a couple of experiences.

One involved Nick Faldo. We had signed Nick to a PGA Tour contract in May of 1998, and he accompanied us on some of our presentations in New York City. The hardhearted brokers of Wall Street were captivated when we held a session at Chelsea Pier and Nick conducted a ball-striking exhibition at the range.

Another memory comes from a presentation we gave at the 21 Club in Manhattan. During my segment, one person grilled me on the fact that I was selling some of my stock in the offering. I was prepared for the question and pointed out that the percentage I was selling was below average for people in my position. He didn't like my answer, and essentially said that if I sold the stock I'd quit working. This bugged me because it was 180 degrees away from my nature, so I went on to explain that as I stood there that not only did I not have a dime to my name, but that technically up to the last year my pay (or lack thereof) qualified me for food stamps. I told him that I could do a much better job if that financial stress were lifted.

After the presentation an attractive woman, well-dressed in business attire, asked if she could speak with me. Her message was succinct: "Mr. Adams, the next time someone asks about you selling stock, just tell them you've earned the right to make that decision." What makes this both funny and memorable was her choice of words. Lets just say I've toned it down considerably.

The road show was a huge success, starting on June 10 and culminating on July 9 with the largest public offering in the history of the golf industry. It would have been a perfect "happily-ever-after" scenario—but it never materialized.

TWENTY-FOUR

SECOND HALF OF 1998, UGLY REALITY

*O*n July 22, 1998, Callaway Golf put out its quarterly report, which contained some chilling news. They said that the golf equipment business was flat and would be that way for the foreseeable future. This announcement was made after the market closed on July 22, 1998, with their stock at $18 a share, and the next day their stock dropped to $12. At the time, Callaway was roughly ten times larger than we were, with twenty years experience in the golf equipment industry. In other words, they were in a position where if we had gained a fraction of their success we'd be very happy. This report came less than two weeks after our public offering. Our quarter after the IPO was the best in our history, but it went virtually unnoticed in the media wave of stories concerning the recession in the equipment business, and our stock price dropped significantly.

I said earlier in the book that we weren't really in the golf equipment business, and that instead we sold unique fairway woods and small quantities of irons and drivers. Our entire system was about opening accounts, and distributing a hot product. We did not have the infrastructure in place to pulse the industry. Callaway did. Furthermore they were the one company Wall Street listened to when it came to golf equipment. At the time they were the only public company that sold just clubs (as opposed to clubs and golf balls), and they were enormously successful. As far as Wall Street was concerned, what they said was gospel.

Callaway's announcement was equivalent to someone putting out the sun. And that darkness created a malaise throughout the golf equipment industry that one could argue still exists today, nine years later.

I'd like to able to write that we braved the storm and continued to enjoy great success despite the negative market. While I'm at it, I might as well also include a lot of other bits of fantasy because that's what it would be. If we had been a mature company at the time, with the proper support structure, we might have been able to put together a survival strategy, something proactive. And in a way I guess we did but it seemed like we were running full speed only to fall farther behind our competition.

In the months that followed, I noticed some things internally at Adams that set off alarms. In those days I never used a computer and did not have one in my office. My practice was management by wandering around. I'd walk the building from management functions to shipping, ostensibly being visible and offering a positive word for everyone. I'll say I was subconsciously looking for WOW events, but it was certainly not part of any formal procedure. All the time I walked I listened carefully, and one thing I picked up was a different atmosphere in our telesales group. Things seemed more strained. I couldn't put my finger on anything specific, but I had a sense that things weren't quite right. And when I asked our VP of sales about it, his answer didn't quite mesh with what my personal radar was telling me.

I wanted more information, so I made some unannounced visits to the retail market. Let me put this into perspective. I sensed that there was a bit of a struggle internally at Adams. We were not in the mainstream of the golf equipment industry and we did not have field sales personnel to give us first-hand customer analysis.

My visits revealed two significant facts that would affect our business for some time. First, the Callaway announcement got the attention of the retailers. They were committed to cutting back inventory, focusing on selling what they had. This caused considerable problems for the large, well-established companies, and they responded with very attractive pricing, terms and, in some cases, renting retail floor space to display their products. This left little money or interest in products from a small company noted particularly for a fairway wood design.

The second lesson was specifically about our area of fairway woods. The competition hadn't taken a nap since the introduction of the Tight Lies in 1996. Instead, they looked at our features and benefits and came up with good competitive models. As I was visiting customers (incognito, of course) I would tell the various salespeople on the floor that I was looking for a new fairway wood. I'd tell them that I had heard about the Tight Lies and wondered if they carried it. Invariably, the salespeople would respond by telling me that the did carry the Tight Lies, but that in my best interest I should really look at brand X, Y, or Z instead. Initially this shocked me—this was our market, our expertise. Upon further inquiry I was told the competing model was superior, hitting ten or twenty yards longer (distance being the holy grail of performance). I knew the claims were exaggerated at the least, but that wasn't really the issue. The issue was figuring out why were we no longer the favored club and why this information wasn't the focal concern at Adams Golf.

Again, at the end of the day, it was about money. Our competitors knew our prices and the margin we offered retailers, and simply competed by offering better deals. Further, they offered incentives to the floor sales personnel—everything from sales contests to an industry practice called spiffs, which pays a cash bonus for every club sold. They made the floor sales personnel part of their team. This was an excellent, intelligent way to compete. It was perfectly legal, practiced in other industries, but not by Adams Golf.

In retrospect, this one was my fault. My reaction was to the product. I knew how good it was, and our competitors' spurious claims consumed my thought process. I wasn't alone here, either. Callaway sued a company, Orlimar, because of what they deemed misleading product comparison claims on fairway woods, and got a decision to their satisfaction. Given the view from 2008, I can think of several things I could have done then to compete more favorably. While I'm convinced these moves would have had some degree of success, I can't be certain. Solutions are always easier to come by when you're looking back.

This does not mean that nothing happened. Quite the contrary. It wasn't like we sat and wrung our hands. A few weeks after my field excursions and some time for thought, I sat down with Mark Gonsalves, our VP of sales and a key figure in our growth, to map out a new strategy for Adams.

I explained to Mark that I had made a series of quiet visits to a variety of customers and reviewed what I observed. I told him that our telesales plan, the key to our successful marketing strategy, needed changing. I felt that it was time to start using field sales representatives and a more traditional sales organization. Mark did not agree. He felt that the infomercial, which we still ran regularly, was a negative for some key retailers. He thought we could establish the necessary customer relationships with the telesales group and customer visits he made. It was not a rancorous discussion, but it became clear that we saw our future growth evolving in significantly different ways. After more discussions he eventually decided to leave Adams Golf, not because of our different views (although that must have been a factor), but because our success had made him a visible commodity and he had an opportunity in another company (not golf-related) that he couldn't afford to ignore.

When Mark announced he was leaving, I had to find a replacement. I'd had a sense Mark was unhappy and had done a little poking around before he notified me of his decision. First, I combed the golf industry, not to hire a VP of sales but to start someone who would eventually become my replacement. But, unable to find the kind of person I was looking for within the industry, I decided to hire someone from outside it, a decision that, at the time, was questioned by some of my board members.

I knew Chip Brewer as a young, well-educated guy who had succeeded in a variety of functions in a company outside the golf industry. I knew he was looking to join a small company, perhaps even a start-up. Further, I learned that he had started as a shift foreman straight out of graduate school. Having also started as a shift foreman, I related to him and his willingness to start at a not-so-glamorous level. He was also an excellent golfer who had been around the game all his life and played at the collegiate level. My decision to hire Chip was criticized because some of my board would have preferred that I bring in an industry star. I didn't share their view. I still saw us as a small entrepreneurial company and felt we needed someone who would thrive in that atmosphere.

Around the time of Chip's hire (September 1998), we also hired a head of R&D, Scott Burnett, an experienced engineer who *did* come from a large equipment company. Even before the IPO, we were taking steps to build an R&D department. The objective was to keep introducing series of easy-to-hit, innovative products for golfers of all skill levels. Now, with an industry professional at the helm, we were prepared to make the investment needed to optimize this process.

We had Nick Faldo on staff starting in May of 1998, and he was a great help participating in our road show. We told everyone that it was going to be a combination of his knowledge as one of the greatest players in the game and our engineering efforts that would produce superior product. Initially we got off to a good start with the Faldo wedges, which we promoted through an infomercial with modest success

As we entered 1999 the relationship between Adams and Nick soured. Nick was precise and very demanding when it came to golf equipment, and since I was still fairly involved in the details of the business I took this as a good thing, figuring that it made us better. Along the way his personal game began to deteriorate as tournament golf was changing from a precision game to a power game. Nick was a precision player, and when he started to struggle he also lost interest in playing our new club designs.

When a golfer has had great success (like Faldo had) and is failing to perform at a high level, often the mindset is to go back and recapture the time when he was successful. That may mean playing the irons or woods you won with in the past. As a golfer myself, I completely understand this, but in my position at Adams I couldn't allow it to happen. We at Adams were about going forward and, if Nick ignored all the products, our message would be mixed at best. What Nick wanted us to do was not to create a new set of irons but to copy his old set and put our name on it. This was a practice not uncommon in the golf industry, and if some inquisitive writer asked about the clubs they were always referred to as "prototypes." We did not consider that approach, however, as it did not meet with the goals of the company.

Nick had a contract with us. We felt the spirit wasn't followed, and that's when lawyers got involved. After months of negotiations, we finally reached a solution. Except for an occasional strong showing, Nick never regained his former status. It's not that we supplied him with bad product, either. He never switched. Looking back at both sides of the issue, I'd say our relationship was doomed from the beginning. Despite the legal issues, his manager at that time, John Simpson, remains a good friend. Today Nick is successfully working as a TV commentator, and this success comes as no surprise. I spent a fair amount of time with him and saw a side of Nick Faldo that is perfect for that environment.

Given the pricing and considerations from the major companies, I knew we were going to have an extremely difficult time expanding into irons and drivers. In the face of that uncertainty I did the only thing I knew: I worked harder. We struggled through the second half of 1998 and prepared for '99 with new, innovative products. What else could we have done? This is the stuff of case studies, and from the position of pure hindsight it makes for many interesting conversations.

TWENTY-FIVE

1999 TO 2000, THE END OF THE BARNEY ERA

*O*ur goal was to build brand recognition and to supplement that effort with innovative new products. Chip Brewer was now running the sales effort, and he was in the process of putting full-time reps in the field, supplemented by a support staff. We hired a very professional advertising agency, and I continued the process of developing the infrastructure of a real company. Once again, I'd like to report brilliant decisions resulting in smashing successes, and once again, well … you know. On balance, we did do the right things. Certainly my friend, the Monday morning quarterback, and I can point out areas where we could have done much better. By itself that is a silly exercise; history is there and you can use it to preclude making the same mistakes twice. There are few circumstances where hindsight cannot find some errors if that is the only goal.

The golf equipment business is a zero-sum game. To compete, you have to introduce and sell dynamic new products every year. Essentially, the selling year builds from January (in the warm weather areas), peaks in the summer, and starts to drop off in the fall and winter. This is because accounts sell their inventories to generate cash for the next year's dynamic new products. Once the new year starts, you're back at zero and you must perform all over again. With the Tight Lies club, we went from hearing our customers say, "Please come see me," to "What are you going to do next?"

I've researched a lot of this information, looking at old memos and talking to key employees who are still with us. No one said so, but one conclusion I drew in this effort is that I was wearing down personally. I've never been a great believer in the effects of stress, but there are shelves of books about stress and its effect on business. Sure, sometimes it's tough, but you sign on for that when you take the job, the responsibility, and the money. I know I'm old-school, but to me blaming stress is too much like blaming bad behavior today on unpleasant incidents from childhood. I'm not talking about serious stuff like mental illness; I'm talking about taking responsibility for one's actions. If you're so stressed that you feel you need time in a non-stress environment where you can recharge your batteries, consider the guy who works in a factory to support his family. He uses most of his vacation time to make extra money. What about his stress? I can hear my psychologist friend, Dr. Coop, saying, "Adams, nobody can look so foolish as when they pretend expertise in a field where they have none." With that in mind, I'll shut up. Enough said.

Indicative of my wearing down were some of the memos that I wrote then. Rereading them recently, I actually had to check and be sure they were really mine despite seeing my signature on all of them. They didn't sound like me and they weren't written by a person I would have liked very much. At the time I was thinking about our challenges every waking moment and making every effort I felt was applicable. Whether the decisions I made at the time were good or questionable, it's my observation today that the original Barney had changed.

I have written and will continue to write about my mistakes and how you can avoid them. For a change, what follows is a case in which I think we did things right, and the result was still a disaster. The great lesson to take away here is that no matter how thoroughly you plan, the results can stink. Keep a close eye and be flexible.

We needed an internal IT network to help us manage our growth. I was not computer-oriented, and in this case I figured my specific ignorance would be an asset. I knew that we had to share data because for years I'd been personally involved with the functions, doing them by hand. Take just one of a dozen situations that needs coordination. You have an order: customer name, address, shipping location, and required date. Time is critical, so you work overtime and, with a sigh of relief, see the order ship as scheduled. After this is done, you come upon another source of information that tells you this particular customer is months behind in paying his bills, and as long as you are dumb enough to keep shipping to him he's a happy camper.

Add in our geometric growth factor, and the need for an internal network is obvious. So I interviewed, researched, and hired, an IT consultant. As insurance, our CFO, Daryl Hatfield, came from KPMG, a big-eight accounting firm with a division that chose and installed IT systems, so we included that company in the process as well. We had employee meetings asking what each person would like in a system, and we developed a wish list in order of importance. I could go on, but my role was to get the proper people involved, make sure our requests were legitimate and clearly defined, then step aside and let the experts take over.

An unmitigated disaster followed: a system that partially worked, that was worse than doing it by hand, and that took a good three years to effectively become a working system.

I've tried to understand this fiasco better, and have had several conversations with CEOs about it when attending various business functions. While it remains something of a mystery, I can choose from the following scenarios. One, despite all my precautions, I either picked the wrong supplier or communicated poorly at the beginning. Two, it was a problem influenced by the times and the lack of maturity in the IT industry.

Why do I mention this IT mess? First, to prepare you for the knowledge that no matter how well you plan something it can go seriously wrong; second, to talk a little about WOW. I can guarantee that the company that supplied the system was not infused with a WOW philosophy (and they are a major company in the field). If they were, it was several software revisions down the road. Monday-morning quarterback and I would have personally gone to some of their customer installations and looked for WOW. We sent the experts, but they only saw mistakes they knew they could fix, being experts and all. The last reason I write specifically about the IT disaster is because I'm still mad about it. I really, really, tried to do it in a correct manner, and failed miserably. Maybe writing about it will be therapeutic.

One of the reasons the system failed is that it was initially difficult to operate. The very people who supplied the criteria had to undergo serious training, and that whole process was doomed from the beginning. User-friendly turned out to mean user-friendly only to the experts.

I said at the outset that not being computer-savvy myself could have been an asset in the process, and given hindsight I was correct. Instead of being impressed by the great capability of the system I should have paid a lot more attention to basic adaptability concerning our people—not what will work but what *does* work with relative simplicity, now. How can I use the words simplicity and computers in the same sentence? A two-word answer! good engineering. In my little world, good engineering doesn't mean great potential—it means thoughtful application, so the "hands-on" users, can adapt quickly.

Here's an area where the industry does a number on you. Unless you keep buying the upgrades, you can't get service. They use the latest, which only interfaces with the latest, which means you have to upgrade... Get the picture?

I was fishing in Alaska a few years ago and met a very nice couple who traveled about looking for optimum fishing opportunities. I asked about his business and it turned out he owned a very successful company. They contracted with businesses in the throes of IT disasters like the one we had experienced and got them back to operational. He regaled me for hours with stories; I laughed through my tears because they all could have been about us.

We needed a PGA Tour presence after the end of the Nick Faldo relationship, and in mid-1999 I got a call from Tom Watson's agent, Chuck Rubin. Tom had been with Ram Golf, but its demise and subsequent sale left him without an equipment sponsor. We were aware of that when his agent called. He said that Tom had always liked our woods but didn't know if we made irons.

Let me explain some things about tour representation. If you see a player carrying a bag on tour from an equipment company, he might be playing with fourteen clubs from that manufacturer, or he might be playing only one. He might be playing clubs the company sells, or he might be playing a special set made just for him. Tom wanted to represent a company; moreover, he wanted to play what they made and sold, so his question was, "Do you guys make irons?" As it turned out, I was holding an iron in my hands when the call came. It was a prototype for a new model, one we felt would be applicable to the best players. I told this to Tom's agent and he asked me to send it up so Tom could give it a try.

There was no way that club was going without me, so I arranged to meet Tom in Kansas City. I brought a club with me, a prototype seven iron. Tom was ready when we met, and we rode in a cart to the back of the range. He told me he wanted to hit twenty to thirty shots with his own seven iron, and then repeat the procedure with ours. It was just me, Tom, and a shag bag full of new balls. No caddie, no electronics.

He proceeded to hit what I saw as thirty perfect shots with his club—different heights, soft draws, fades—and I figured it was over. I've been playing golf for fifty years, and I just saw an array of perfect shots. He then took our club and hit thirty more perfect shots in the same pattern, turned to me, and said, "Barney, your club was very easy to work. I can play with this." He then proceeded to ask me a few technical questions, and later he explained that he had wanted to know the depth of my understanding. I guess my answers passed muster.

I was in his presence for maybe forty minutes, including rounding up the balls. We shook hands and I headed back to Dallas. Shortly thereafter, his agent came to Dallas and we worked out a deal that marked the beginning of a wonderful relationship. I am very proud to report that since day one Tom has played all Adams clubs (except his putter) and has been a wonderful spokesman for the company. I'm told that this was one of my easiest decisions, but at the time that was not the case. I was the one who had picked Faldo, and it had not worked out; that failure did not go unnoticed or uncriticized, and that's as it should be. Certainly I knew Tom Watson as a great player, but would he be a benefit to the company? Fortunately, the answer was and is a resounding yes. There is always an element of luck in making a decision like hiring Tom, but I prefer to credit his character. I also like to think that somehow I intuited that.

All the management changes were not over. Chip Brewer was doing a good job in sales and made it clear that he thought he could perform equally well as company president. I agreed with him, but this was July of 2000, a scant two years after the road show. I never stated that I was going to be there forever, but neither did I plan to replace myself within two years.

I discussed the situation with the group who were our major shareholders; between us, we controlled the voting stock of the company. They were great, telling me that they had been with me since day one and would back any decision I made. If I decided to stay as president, they understood that it was a possibility that Chip might leave. "Barnyard," they told me, "this ball is squarely in your court. It's a major decision, so think it through."

The process was complex. The company hadn't performed well after the IPO. I was the leader, and I take the consequences. This is not my opportunity to tell everyone how the industry decline made it virtually impossible to grow a new company; that argument is not applicable. The question is, given the assets at my disposal, did I perform to a level that warranted staying on in my current position? A significant part of me felt that I could stay, continue to improve things, and leave on a better note; furthermore, I wanted to stay.

In this analysis no one was harder on me than I was. My personal, post-IPO report card was not showing an exemplary performance. Sure, industry conditions were a major factor, but the really good guys come through in all conditions. This was my company; was I too close to it, to all the people, and therefore slow to make critical decisions? I asked several knowledgeable friends, and every conversation ended with them telling me that it was my call. I changed my mind at least a dozen times and finally came to the conclusion that it was time for new blood at the top. Chip Brewer was named president of Adams Golf shortly thereafter.

Chip came on, did a great job, things improved immediately, and ... oops, wrong story. Instead, he had the pleasure of encountering negative momentum. It's one of the toughest things to overcome in business and, because of it, Adams continued to struggle. Chip made tough decisions on internal personnel and operating systems.

Scott Burnett, our head of R&D, had been recruited away by a major equipment company. Chip hired Tim Reed, a well-respected industry veteran, as VP of R&D and started making significant investments in that area. In retrospect, I see this as one of Chip's best moves—not only the hiring of Tim but the willingness to make a significant investment into what is now the largest department in the company.

Earlier in the book I referenced the zero-sum nature of the golf equipment industry. Regardless of the previous year, sales start each year essentially at zero, and the company has to perform all over again. Introducing new products is not a case of unique ideas every year, but of building on what you know. Your R&D department builds a database compiling countless variations on shape, weight distribution, and other factors, and then compares historic test results and consumer reactions. You introduce your new designs to tour players and gauge their reactions as well. Most tour players are not graduate engineers by degree, but they have hit thousands of golf balls and you learn to respect and note their reactions to a club.

All of this accumulated knowledge goes into making the next generation of products better or more consumer-friendly. In the highly competitive world of club design, this process is critical. For Mr. Golf Ball the important things are strictly physical properties, but clubs are a consumer product. Industrial design experts work on eye appeal. They coordinate with marketing on how the product will be presented, with all of this requiring a team of highly skilled, experienced people. All of these efforts are about recognizing that the company's future is dependent on innovative products that are easy to hit, and without Chip's investment in R&D we could never have competed.

Chip fiercely guarded our cash, with the position that the company would not take on any debt. Time passed and his decisions started to have a positive effect, despite predictions to the contrary by many "industry experts." The company survived, and Chip was named president and CEO in 2002.

I am a non-executive CEO, which means I perform some ceremonial duties but am not involved with the day-to-day operations of the company anymore. This does not mean my mind has disappeared, and I'm not shy about offering opinions on various aspects of the business as I see them. They are just that—opinions. I strongly suspect they will continue to show up in my e-mails, and I'm positive that Chip looks forward to every one of them.

Recently I was asked an interesting question in the Q&A session of a seminar, referencing the management change at the top. The question was, "Barney, how did you react after the change?" My response was to smile and quip, "Not well." But for those in the business world this question is worth further discussion.

I started Adams in 1987 and decision time came in 2000. I spent the equivalent of more than twenty years pouring every ounce of energy I had into the business. I say more than twenty years because for me the job was in play every waking moment, whether I was physically in our building, on the range, or anyplace else, as long as I was awake, and by 2000 I was wearing down. I even kept a notepad by my bed to record the brilliant ideas that woke me during the night, which happened often. The ideas happened, anyway, not the brilliant part. I have no recollection of any particular results from that process.

My first reaction immediately following my decision to step aside was a desire to help, and that was wrong. If I went to the employees and explained that Chip was taking over and I was simply trying to make it seamless, I created a problem. It was Adams Golf, and I was the founder. I'd done virtually every job in the building and, no matter how honorable my intentions, all I did was get in the way. When I was around, people related to me as they had done for years, and I was making the transition harder, not easier.

I understand the reaction from the outside: "Gee, poor Barney, he's forced to play golf, go fishing, travel, isn't life unfair." And they are 100 percent right. But as much as I understood that from an intellectual perspective, it still bothered me tremendously on an emotional level.

One day I was talking with Dr. Coop, my psychologist friend, and after we analyzed North Carolina basketball I confessed that I was really depressed. This feeling was made worse by having the appearance of a life with no cares. He explained that while the obvious answer was to find things to do, I needed to have some projects that required a creative input. His advice included the technical reason why, but I won't bore you with those details. Suffice it to say that he was correct, and you're reading one of the projects.

So, the good advice from Dr. Coop and the great equalizer, father time, helped me adjust. I go out of my way to praise the job done at Adams post-Barney, and those running the company deserve every favorable word I can muster. Does this mean I agree with all their decisions? No. Does this mean I don't think I could jump in where needed? Of course I do. As written before, this isn't fiction. So how did I react? Not well initially, but okay over time.

Another of Chip's good decisions was the emphasis on association with players on the Senior (now Champions) Tour. In the world of golf marketing, the PGA Tour is the proverbial big dog. Their players get all the big endorsement contracts, basically for one reason—television exposure. Essentially, as a sponsor you pay to get your name on television; the more the exposure, the more it costs. A small company like Adams in 2000 has no business competing on the PGA Tour unless it has a large corporate owner who understands the validity of a five- to seven-year marketing plan with the tour as the basis.

Chip and his team turned their attention to the Senior Tour, which, while affordable, was a considerable gamble. First, at the time, it was showing on CNBC with a cable audience of four to six viewers. Second, there was (and to some degree is) a ridiculous perception on behalf of the golfing public that the players were seniors, a bunch of has-beens with no game left, and certainly not a group to look to for inspiration on equipment choices.

As the Senior Tour moved to the Golf Channel and changed its name to the Champions Tour, the public learned what we had known all along: that they were still great players, way beyond the skill levels of the best amateurs. The Adams marketing strategy started working for a variety of reasons, and I'll list three.

The first is exposure. As the broadcasting moved to the Golf Channel, the public became more exposed to the skill levels involved.

Second, is Max Puglielli, my old buddy from the Haney Ranch, who runs all the tour reps, but is based on the Champions Tour. A trained club-fitter who brings great passion to his job, Max is also a fascinating person, conversant in five languages, and a gourmet cook. On every personal visit to the Champions Tour, I meet players who praise Max as the finest tour staff person they have ever worked with, and they all mention his knowledge and dedication.

Third, is the development of new products, primarily hybrid technology, which was embraced by Champions Tour players. As I write, Adams holds the number-one position in overall tour usage, combining the PGA, Champions, and Nationwide Tours.

Currently the company is investing in sponsoring LPGA players, and while branching out is good business, it brings a new world of discomfort. Golf will always have a macho side; the long hitters get more headlines. I realize it's a Wal-Mart mentality—how many could be built between my drives and theirs. But the final injustice is sending me to grab my fishing rods. "Barney," they'll say, "We'd like you to meet our latest LPGA Tour staff player," and out will step a very attractive, polite young charmer who has me wishing I was forty years younger, and then WHACK. She nails a tee shot I couldn't reach with a hurricane behind me hitting to an asphalt-hard fairway.

It used to be said that 50 percent of the men would gain knowledge by watching the women's slower but excellent swings. That's now about 99 percent. There is a remarkable skill level on the LPGA Tour.

I'm proud that Adams is recognized as an innovative company with its leadership in hybrid technology, and that its new products continue to win awards from industry analysts. It still has no debt, and is in a good cash and inventory position. R&D is now a team of twenty-seven and growing as I write, a far cry from me, the range, and a yellow pad for notes. I love to go in and just watch the degree of sophistication. As advanced as they are, looking is about all I can do. I suspect some of the new R&D people wonder who the old guy wandering around is. I keep waiting for security to politely ask me if they can be of assistance.

I still get calls from the media wanting to know about Adams in the "old" days. My objective when taking these calls is to turn the emphasis to the folks running the place today and their outstanding performance. The company jockeys between the number-three and number-four positions in total iron sales, behind giants Callaway and TaylorMade. You might ask what the big deal is about being #3, and my answer is to look at all the major brands we have passed. It's been a great team effort, and if applicable I'd name every member.

Now with this book I'll have told the full story as I move into the section dedicated specifically to golf equipment. The company continues to do well and the public financial results confirm their efforts. It will always be an ongoing battle, with victories accompanied by innovative new products that make the great game more fun to play.

There are two final chapters in this section, and they are dedicated in a general sense to the WOW factor. I struggled with their presentation if for no other reason than I did not embrace WOW in a formal sense. Maybe someone will read this and come up with a way of integrating WOW into a corporate culture. That would be a very good thing.

TWENTY-SIX

WOW AND THE CORPORATE CULTURE

I mentioned earlier that I struggled in naming the book *The WOW Factor*. I was worried that the title sounded too much like one of those pop management systems, a cutesy title to attract interest. But WOW was a real event, and one that helped me through some difficult times. Further, it is alive today and part of the culture at Adams Golf, though not in a formal sense.

WOW is simple and complex at the same time; you can run a company on WOW, or use it to design a product. To explain that apparent contradiction, I'll start by reliving my own experience. If you get a sense of déjà vu, it's because I talked about this briefly in chapter seventeen. I was working on the driving range of a teaching facility, the Hank Haney Golf Ranch, from 3:00 P.M. to 9:00 P.M. about six days a week. I started each day by going to our small manufacturing facility where we designed, assembled, and shipped golf clubs. The product was good, but essentially no one cared. Each afternoon, I headed to the range, where I custom-fit golfers for their clubs. The fittings produced enough sales to stay in business, and it was the service, the process of fitting, that made the sale.

In my club-fitting process I was frustrated by not having the proper tools (clubs) to optimize results for my customers. Remember, my goal was optimum ball flight, not just doing the best job with what I had. My fix was to design a particular club that, while looking much different than traditional products of the time, was engineered to accomplish one particular function: to get the ball into the air easily and quickly. When I received my first design samples and gave them to golfers of all abilities to hit, the one constant I heard was, "WOW, this is really good." This was not said to me directly. Instead, it was a verbal reaction to hitting the club. I was dealing with golfers who had tons of data in their mental storage, and when they first hit the Tight Lies their instinctive response was, "WOW."

At the time this was just something I observed and filed in my own mental storage bin. It was critical because, as we tried to market the club, reactions from industry experts (all the smart people) were hardly promising. It's a bit difficult to put this in perspective. I had customers calling me to buy the product, but they had to go out of their way to find us. I thought that the product must have great potential, yet everywhere I went to find an industry partner I got turned down. I am not saying the theory of WOW was something I constantly thought about and used to keep the product alive at that time. What actually happened was conflict between what experts were telling me and what I had experienced firsthand. It was only after the Tight Lies became successful, after all the experts said they knew it was good all along, that I examined what impetus kept us going. Was it luck? Some. Bullheadedness? Certainly. But there had to be more, and I kept coming back to the WOW experience.

Ever go on a trip where someone says something and it becomes a mantra, gets repeated in a variety of situations? So it was with WOW. It became part of our company, and one of my regrets is that I didn't do a better job of formally integrating it into our daily operations.

We have all had WOW experiences with products and services. You can think of them as you read these words, but how would you incorporate the philosophy into your company? It may seem easy, even simplistic, but it isn't.

The difficulty and beauty of properly applied WOW is that it automatically regenerates. Isn't it obvious that you must follow one WOW with another? That becomes the challenge. Take an example we're all familiar with—a restaurant. You go there, have a great dinner, enjoy excellent service, and it's truly a WOW experience. The next time you go back it's as if the place had changed. It's simply not as good. Is it possible your expectations were too high? Sure. But isn't it also possible that the establishment wasn't committed to WOW, and that what you experienced was inconsistency on their part? Either way, the restaurant probably lost a customer.

The arena of today's electronic devices is a WOW world. It's relatively young, the technology expands geometrically, and the market base grows annually. Take one of my favorite devices, the iPod. I consider that a WOW product, and its later editions have met the challenge of following a WOW introduction with further WOW improvements.

The greatest WOW of our times is, of course, the Internet, (honorable mention to GPS technology), and because of its scope and complexity I will make no effort to write about it. I watch the Net, I wonder about values, I wonder about the effects of creative destruction, and I wonder how they can keep giving away things that appear to me to be the result of some very creative work. Far better researchers than I have done excellent work on this subject, so among hundreds of literary choices I'll plug Thomas Friedman's excellent *The World is Flat* and let the matter rest.

Let's turn the clock back to Adams. We had a WOW with the Tight Lies, and since I was still in charge and therefore responsible,

I'll say that the next generation wasn't WOW. We tried our best, but the process of continuation is very difficult. Today the company has hybrids, which are definitely a WOW product. They have followed the initial success with improved hybrid technology integrated throughout the set, an effort that yielded a pure WOW performance.

Let me provide a specific example of the difficulty involved in a continuation of WOW. I was enjoying one of my infrequent visits to Adams and, as is my habit, gravitated to the R&D area. We were talking about hybrids, and one of the engineers commented on the difficulty of designing new generations. I inquired as to why, and the answer was very interesting. Original hybrids replaced long irons, which was a no-brainer. The two, three, and even four iron for most golfers is difficult to hit efficiently, and the hybrid is a godsend to them. As the line matures we found ourselves designing for everyone, especially the slower swing speed players—seniors and women—which is a big market.

They're also not stupid, and most gave up the long irons in favor of seven, nine, and eleven woods, which they hit well and liked very much. As a designer, the objective is then to provide a WOW for clubs that well may be the players' favorites, as opposed to long irons, which definitely were not. You can't win this game unless you identify the challenge and undertake the difficult task it presents. This market represents the majority of golfers, so you can either try and ride your earlier success with creative marketing or accept the challenge from a design and performance perspective. This isn't easy, and that's my point. WOW sounds like fun, but in reality it is a serious challenge.

This little story is absolutely essential as an example of commitment to WOW as a philosophy. It means constant assessment. You must always be asking, who is the WOW for? What is it up against? I'm proud to say that the Adams R&D folks understood this and have met a very difficult challenge as they continue to develop new advances in hybrid technology.

In the case of the iPod, initially it was up against nothing, and the criteria for WOW was that it perform as advertised, an objective that not all new products meet. Subsequent versions had to offer improved performance and features compared to the original, which as a consumer I feel they have accomplished.

Decades ago there was a theory known as "planned obsolescence," wherein a new product, say a home appliance, was designed to give out after a certain amount of usage, sending customers scurrying for the latest version with all its WOW features and benefits. Interestingly, this "nature abhors a vacuum" competitive environment opened the door for well-engineered products designed to last a lifetime, supported by strong warranties. That's one of the things I really like about WOW; from a product standpoint there is absolutely no room for less than good—really good.

If you are motivated by this thought process and you want to be sure WOW is incorporated into your products, I say think again. You cannot do so effectively unless you are committed to the same philosophy in your business methods.

Pick any area of your business and challenge your people to be a WOW group. Ask them what it would take, and be sure you are personally capable of supplying the proper support. If, as you read this, you're struck by inspiration—by gosh, your company, restaurant, dry cleaners, whatever, is going to become a WOW business—some day you'll write and thank me. (I prefer wine.)

Desire for WOW is great, but you must have a balanced management style to make it work. The micromanager won't enlist a team effort, and the guy with Title-itis will announce WOW in a meeting, retreat to his office, and take credit if things somehow fall into place. Either way, you can stop budgeting for my wine purchase, because it isn't going to happen.

Whether it's finance, marketing, customer service, sales—whatever area of your business you pick—you need to first determine what will make it a WOW area. I can tell you from experience that you probably don't have the answer. Ask your employees and you will probably find that they don't either, at least not for the company overview. It's going to take some work, usually a lot of work, because WOW must be a congruent strategy. What one department may think of as WOW might be completely upsetting to another.

One time when I was speaking with our collections people I tried to ascertain what they considered to be a WOW environment. It turned out what they thought was perfect was a software-supported system that kept them informed up-to-the-minute on the account status of every customer. Included in the database would be names and phone numbers so staff could personally be on top of every situation, calling accounts as soon as they reached any credit limitation.

When I mentioned this to the sales guy, I had to watch him roll on the floor and foam at the mouth. Finally, I extracted a tearful explanation that a WOW approach in that vein would disrupt his sales force and their efforts to establish working relationships with their customers. He wasn't advocating financial irresponsibility, but his world was one where his people were face-to-face with their customers and they needed to create a positive relationship. Calls from credit had to be a last resort and carefully planned. The issue was eventually resolved, and what I'm pointing out is that the WOW objective is much more complex than it may appear.

If you are a micromanaging type, you'll spend endless time solving the sales/collections issue, finally dictating what WOW is. Not their version, your version. If you suffer from Title-itis, you'll throw out the concept and wait for the issues to work themselves out. If everything works out, well, you'll take credit. If it doesn't, it was "their" fault.

If you really want to establish WOW as something central to your working culture, you, the big dog, are going to have to communicate, listen, and most important, be in a position to support. You get honorable mention as a good manager by introducing the WOW factor, but where you really earn your plaudits (and big bonus) is being the type of manager who allows the philosophy to work. In so doing, understand one thing: not everyone cares! You may be infused with the WOW philosophy, but I promise there are some people in your company who are only there for the check and really care more about some personal hobby or passion of theirs than committing themselves to WOW. This is normal. It will always be the case, and there's nothing wrong with it. Your team's goal is to incorporate the WOW philosophy in such a way that by doing their jobs, all employees are contributing. You cannot expect the same enthusiasm from everyone, because that's unrealistic. But this is one area where you and your key managers get to excel.

It's easy to talk about WOW regarding products, their design, and quality manufacturing, but how do you extend that message throughout the manufacturing force? I can give one example in which everyone, regardless of job, education, and experience, can participate: housekeeping. Install a culture of a clean facility and good work habits and you're installing WOW. I've had visitors come to our place and comment on how clean it was, and we hadn't shut down and prepared. That wasn't the WOW, though. The WOW came when one of our manufacturing group leaders told me he heard about the visitors' reaction and how it made the employees proud.

One easy approach to incorporating WOW into your business from a sales perspective is to go to your customers. You know your customer base far better than I do, so I'll focus this discussion on selling to retail where I have the experience. What is a WOW for your customer is easy to identify: a great product with consumer demand and good margins (okay, *great* margins). Pretty obvious, right? The honest answer is, maybe. Let's say you have all of the ingredients, especially a terrific product line and tremendous demand, but along the way your on-time shipments start missing dates. Your product is still good, as is the quality of your service. You just have a problem coordinating your shipments on time.

When that happens, billing is automatically messed up. You send the bill because your terms are thirty days, as agreed. The only problem is, that's supposed to be thirty days from delivery of the correct product. Finance thinks that's what happened because the billing information is confirming, but the customer's finance department doesn't agree because they got the product wrong or late. After a few such mistakes, you end up with a contentious relationship. Your sales force and their customer relations people provide some assistance, but business issues prevail.

Because the WOW of the product line hasn't extended through the full cycle of doing business, as always the weakest link becomes the issue. Maybe sales and management got a little busy congratulating themselves about their WOW products. Maybe a hundred things went wrong.

All I'm saying here, in a simplistic example that I lifted from a real-world experience, is that to really be a WOW operation every facet of your business must be coordinated. The company in my example lost market share while the products were still good. I can think of many examples, as, I'm sure, can you.

Let me use this forum to issue a WOW challenge. I have a personal dislike for automated phone-answering systems. One could say they are the anti-WOW. I'm not going into the cost/benefit analysis, but I'll concede that in some cases they are necessary. What I will do is issue a WOW challenge. Instead of just buying a system off the shelf or having it designed by Barney Nerdlink, whose contact with the outside world is through his collection of video games, try a different approach. Design a system that, when using it, people say to themselves, "WOW, that is the best automated system I've ever used. I wish everyone would do that." For those hiding in the corner office who think that's a silly idea, what I think is nuts is your ad budget factored by your automated answering system. You spend a ton to market your product, and if the effort is successful, I call, ready to be your customer. When I do, you then expose me to a system that turns me away, just for some cost savings. How does *that* offer your prospective customers a WOW experience?

I'm sure you noticed that this chapter doesn't include any formulas or formal ways to introduce WOW into your thinking or your company. You know your business, and you have, or are developing, people as assets. WOW is a group effort. It is a culture, and for the life of me I can't imagine anyone saying, "No, I don't want my business to have a WOW factor."

TWENTY-SEVEN

ESTABLISHING THE ROOTS OF WOW

One of the folks who read an early draft of this book suggested that I give some advice on how to integrate WOW and the entrepreneurial spirit into a large company environment. Much has been written about entrepreneurship, given the many opportunities that face us today. There are applicable college courses, even advanced degrees to be attained. But if you had asked me what my profession was years ago, I would have said I made golf clubs, not that I was an entrepreneur. I was just trying to make enough to eat while pursuing a goal with great passion.

Looking back there were some positive things we did (the roots of WOW), but it wasn't part of any specific plan. I'm not going to write how to specifically infuse WOW into a large corporate culture. I think good practices are universal and if you find something applicable, feel free to give it a shot.

Being loved as a boss is not a first step. If that's your goal, you'll fail. There are just too many times you'll have to make decisions that will please some and make others unhappy. If you're worried about being loved, your decision-making will suffer. Be consistent and fair and, as arcane as it may sound, the golden rule is a pretty good guideline.

I wanted to make Adams a place where we were dedicated to making innovative golf products that were easy to hit by players of all skill levels. I also wanted to make it a place where people enjoyed the work experience and functioned as a team. I have a distaste for political infighting and am a fan of performance. To some degree this is naïve. No matter what I want, human nature is a powerful force and any attempt to foster a culture may conflict with its basic tenets. This is particularly applicable when attempting to change the momentum of a corporate environment.

I felt that the first step in the our process was an attempt to level the financial playing field. It's off-putting when the boss is running around preaching teamwork and pulling together when his potential financial reward is one hundred times greater than everyone else's. That's why we instituted stock options and perfor-mance bonuses in an attempt to give everyone a chance for relative financial gain.

I have to admit I've been surprised when old conservative Barnyard has been accused of being some kind of new-age liberal. "Hey, you're giving them jobs. That's enough." Allow me to respectfully disagree.

We had an office and an adjoining manufacturing area. I strongly encouraged visits by the office staff and management to the manufacturing floor; I just didn't want a we/they environment. Maybe those folks out there didn't all have degrees, but their perfor-mance was critical to our success and I wanted to be sure that was universally understood.

Personally, I wandered. I didn't follow any pattern, but I con-stantly walked the building, talking to everyone, asking everything from "How can I help?" to "Did you see that game last night?" I understood once we started assembling a team that it was my job to help them perform at the highest level, and that I was one of them.

We'd settle on goals that were not necessarily mine or theirs, but ours. Once we agreed that the goals were attainable, it was my primary job to do whatever I could to help my employees achieve them. If I did something that got in the way, they needed to tell me. This approach did not result in some kind of working nirvana. It never does; that's why there are thousands of books on management styles.

No matter how hard you try, some people will come up with goals because they think that's what you want. If you step back and wait for them to be creative, nothing will happen. I specifically remember hiring a guy with industry-acknowledged expertise in an area where we needed assistance. We had a critical function that needed to be defined, developed, and managed, but we did not have the skills in-house. This was a case of doing everything right going in. His references checked out fine, and his job skills and history were exactly what we needed. As a Monday-morning quarterback, nothing in the pre-hire process would have changed, but it turned out to be a complete failure. I worked personally with him for weeks. Then, in case *I* was the problem, I had others work with him. No confrontations; the relationship was always cordial and professional.

There was only one problem. He couldn't do the job. He wanted one of us to develop strict guidelines and procedures in an area where he was the expert. If we would do that, he would then carefully follow them. Obviously if we had those skills we never would have needed him in the first place.

This is a specific example of ingesting what you read and having the ability to understand that nothing is perfect. You'll have goals and applicable systems; the key is the delicate art of managerial balance.

Cost awareness was always a common theme, but you can't make it applicable to everyone else while you and your staff are above such efforts. I read in amazement about institutions laying people off, announcing big cost-saving measures, all while the CEO spends a small fortune redecorating his office. I'll admit to a personal distaste for overnight mail. I used to track it and was constantly amazed at the pattern that emerged. For whatever reasons, that which was expensively sent overnight was rarely opened the next day. Small potatoes, yes, but cost awareness is a series of small decisions that become part of a culture. It really is awareness of all things all the time.

I love the rules and regulations handed down by the finance people designed to keep everyone in line, especially the sales folks. Since I was a field sales guy to begin with, you can give me any system and if I want to beat it, trust me, I will. Guidelines are essential, but the road to cost-effectiveness is cultural.

I made it clear that the practice of "sucking up" was not only discouraged at Adams, but that I considered it a character flaw. On the other hand, I encouraged critical analysis. My charges were always free to question my decisions, with one caveat: they had to be able to offer a solution. Anyone can dislike something and complain, but real team members figure out a better way. One last rule: after noon on Fridays, I didn't want to hear anything negative unless it was something that could be acted on immediately. I'd just take these complaints home with me and brood over the weekend, spoiling my time and being unable to do anything productive or fun until the following Monday.

Speaking of time, I also encouraged Adams employees to go home at the end of the workday, at 5:00 P.M. There are several reasons for this. One is that I wanted them to have a life away from work. I personally didn't, but that didn't mean my hours were a company guideline. Second, I felt the time away was good for healthy thinking. The third is simple: the company was my life, but it was their job. The stakes, financial and emotional, were different for them and it would be unfair to require them to emulate my work habits. And now another disclosure: When they did leave, following my guidelines, I wanted to shout, "Where are you going? There's work to be done!"

You can see that whether you're a small company or large corporation, the steps to establishing an entrepreneurial culture are not entirely dissimilar. Certainly the big company moves more slowly and I suspect would be influenced by superior performance in a department or division as something to be emulated throughout.

Most of the people I've spoken with that want their workplace to be more open are candidates for upper management. They have great intentions to improve the culture when the time comes. Then they get the promotion, the corner office, the perks, the recognition. Trust me, the first reaction of human nature is to keep them.

All the after-hours conversations about team, sharing, and openness that were heartfelt at the time are now in conflict. That's when you hear that "Joe used to be a good guy until he got the big job." I'll assume that the person in my example really wants to make things more entrepreneurial, to invoke a WOW atmosphere, and will make the effort. It's just that he has new responsibilities, new running mates, and the perfectly natural desire to protect what he has attained. If he's really good he will foster an environment in which his team accomplishes goals and feels they are being recognized and rewarded. If the company is a good one, his contribution will be recognized and he'll get the chance to apply it in a broader landscape.

PART TWO

INSIDE THE GOLF
EQUIPMENT INDUSTRY

TWENTY-EIGHT

WRITING ABOUT GOLF EQUIPMENT

I didn't start writing this book with an ending in mind. I just knew that I wanted to tell the story of my involvement with Adams Golf from day one to the present. It is written as advertised, but hopefully also told in a way that makes the reading enjoyable with applicable business advice. I also promised my golfing friends a look into the equipment business, some insight, fun, and some advice that might help them make good club-buying choices. It's a bit of a departure from the Adams Golf story but it's all part of the same landscape.

Writing about golf equipment can be a prelude to boring reading to all but the severely affected. After all, it is about the application of physics, and Richard Feynman aside, the subject does not make for casual reading. I wanted to dedicate a section to equipment, but I also wanted to do the best I could to make it interesting. When I used to conduct seminars for club pros and assistants, my premise was that they would much rather be out playing golf than listening to me. My personal challenge was to make the talk educational and entertaining.

I don't follow the head, shaft, and grip method of talking about golf clubs. There are lots of books or parts of books around that do just that. In the industry, Alastair Cochrane and John Stobbs's *The Search for the Perfect Swing* is still the closest thing to a reference bible that I'm aware of, even though it was published in 1964. That particular book was the published result of a lengthy and detailed study by a British golf organization.

Today's environment for golf club design and manufacture is a new ball game compared to 1964. I'd like to see a modern version of *The Search for the Perfect Swing* published, assisted by the manpower and analysis of a team from a university. This probably will never happen because it doesn't have a huge potential for commercial success, although stranger things have happened.

Whenever I read anything on golf, be it about the swing, course design, or equipment, my first move is to research the author and his or her credentials. Having read the previous twenty-seven chapters, you're already somewhat familiar with mine. I'm not trying to impress anyone, but to establish that what follows should produce reasonable credibility.

I have no idea how many hundreds of books I've read on golf over the last fifty years. Not just books but also magazines, especially old issues. I have a decent personal collection, and whenever I'm around golf books belonging to others or in a library, I'll skim them, in some cases spending the time to do so in depth. Many golf courses have very interesting libraries, and I've been fortunate to meet folks with awesome personal collections. With the exception of some scenes from *Caddyshack*, I've never seen a golf movie I could watch for more than ten minutes, as I am unable to suspend disbelief. But books are another story. Upon reflection, I guess reading books and working as a caddy at age thirteen are where it started for me.

Those of you who are serious golfers probably have stopped into a freestanding shop where clubs are measured. Usually custom fitting is offered, with the use of sensor-based devices. They record swing speed, ball speed, and other significant measurements pertaining to you and the performance of your clubs. At one time you could have stopped into my shop, which was located at the Hank Haney Golf Ranch.

This was pre-Tiger, but even then Hank's reputation and his outstanding staff attracted tour players, aspiring tour players, good amateurs, beginners, men, women, and kids. For some three years I worked that shop, and I mean hands-on. I repaired clubs, custom-fitted, designed a custom-fitting system, and wrote the manual. We had electronic measuring devices for ball flight that were not as sophisticated as today, but that were still very accurate. We had one other invaluable asset: this was a teaching facility, and our job was to augment the teaching effort.

I am not always a huge fan of custom-fitting as I see it performed today. If you go to a range that has fitting clubs from, say, six different manufacturers, I think that's wonderful. What bugs me (because I've done it) is that you can go through fittings with each manufacturer and get significantly different specs for the same person. I liken this to a tailor who lines up suits by six different designers. In one suit you are a 46 long, in another a 42 regular, and so on. It just doesn't work for me. I know the golf industry does not have consistent specs, which could account for some differences, but not to the degree I've seen.

I would be arrogant to say our fitting process was "the one." What I will say is the Haney Ranch was a teaching facility with improved ball flight as the goal. The custom-fitting process had to work hand in hand with, and complement teaching efforts. We could have prescribed a set of specs over the short term that helped offset a golfer's poor swing. But with the player there to take lessons and learn, that would have impeded the process because decent swings would produce poor ball flight. You would have had to swing poorly to make the clubs work, which was not the ideal philosophy in a teaching center.

Over a three-year period I worked with hundreds of golfers, thousands of swings, from tour players to beginners. Before and after that time I designed clubs and designed a shaft. I've tested shafts and clubs on the range with golfers of all skill levels, assembled full sets, even boxed and delivered them. I hold eight product patents. Some were fair ones, and the Tight Lies was a huge commercial success. I bring this up for one point. There is a major difference between designing something and producing an actual product that achieves commercial success.

I've studied the history of golf club design and development, and I've played a little. I've hit good shots, even broken seventy in competition. This is not to imply that I was a great talent (I wasn't), but just to point out that at one time I could play. I've hit one irons and long drives, but now I'm at Social Security age with one of those short, quick swings. I move off the ball and it goes nowhere. In my 58 years of playing golf I've recorded scores in the 60s, 70s, 80s, and 90s. Unfortunately for my ego the latter two comprise current efforts, but despite that there is little doubt that when it comes to ball flight I have a firsthand understanding.

I have also been privy to a situation that is quite unusual. When you read about great ball strikers, very often Ben Hogan, Lee Trevino, and Moe Norman are mentioned as three of the greatest. I only saw Hogan practice and play, but I've spent a considerable amount of time with the other two. This includes watching them hit balls on the range, talking to them about equipment, making clubs for them, and even playing a few holes together.

I've been privileged to do the same with Tommy Bolt, the 1958 U.S. Open Champion, and my objective in all cases was the same: to learn. Sure, I'd have given a lot to have become a better player from the experience, and the only thing that held me back was a lack of talent. I mention Bolt because I used as much of my time with him as I felt was appropriate to learn about Hogan and his views on golf equipment (and I love Tommy's swing). So if Hogan, Trevino, and Norman really are the three best or even in the top ten, I've had great exposure to them.

A lot of folks in the golf industry have done some of these things. Few, if any, have done all of them, and the topper is that my experience goes back over thirty years. I think this gives me a background to discuss equipment.

Before we start on the history of golf club design, there is one fact I'd like you to read and file away. At impact, the club face is in contact with the ball for 0.00045 seconds. Think of hummingbird wing speed or the blink of an eye. When you make contact, by the time the message of impact registers in your brain, the ball is some forty yards away. Hitting a golf ball is a collision between the club head and a round object sitting there minding its own business. No matter how much you yell, implore, or curse, it ignores you. The only thing that matters is the efficiency involved in the energy transfer from the club head to the ball. You have no control once the ball touches the face.

At the moment of impact it's about the club head and the ball; the shaft has done its job and is out of the picture. If you are standing in the middle of the freeway and a semi going a hundred miles per hour hits you, the aerial is not a factor. All of these things are true, whether you are male, female, young, or old—the golf ball doesn't care. This is true now, it was true back in the early days of the game, and it will never change. Now, let's talk equipment.

TWENTY-NINE

THE HISTORY OF GOLF CLUB DESIGN

*C*lub design has a rich history, and I know of no better reference than the two-volume set titled *The Clubmaker's Art*. Written by Jeff Ellis, it's in limited edition, so if you're interested I suggest you start there. These are huge coffee-table books, and I reference them sometimes for enjoyment, sometimes to research one of my pet theories. I have long maintained that there is little that is truly new in visual golf club design. What we have is the application of new materials and manufacturing processes, resulting in upgrades of ideas handed down over the years.

I want to be 100 percent clear: the use of new materials and design techniques has resulted in some great product advances. They are not merely upgrades of designs from another century. There has been a significant improvement in golf club design, which has accelerated in the last decade. At one time it was a process of starting with something that closely resembled a club, be it wood or metal. A skilled artisan would complete the job, making a beautiful product by hand: grinding, shaping, sanding, and finishing. For elite players getting a personal set, this worked well. To turn out thousands of like product, it wasn't the best method. Karsten Solheim of Ping pioneered the method of investment casting. It allowed him to make "near finished" product directly from the mold and introduced a new world of consistently excellent products.

This is not the improvement I reference, although increased sophistication in the manufacturing process is integral to the achievement. Clubs used to be designed as complete sets, be they irons or woods. A driver came with fairway woods that looked very similar except with smaller heads and more lofted faces. Irons were definitely a set. If you looked at a three iron, you pretty much knew what the seven would look like. I can easily remember when the good players played sets. The adventurous ones might play one brand of woods and another brand of irons, but they still played sets. Along the way this started to change from the players' end; they'd have clubs that didn't match the rest visually but performed well and remained in the bag.

Manufacturers adapted to this by making a variety of specialty clubs for specific situations, but essentially sets (especially irons) were still the norm. The process of designing irons with computer technology was set-driven; you designed key clubs, generally the four and eight iron, and with a keystroke the rest of the set filled out.

Think of it as a formula. A set of irons comes in different lengths, lofts, head weights, and lie angles (I'll skip grips in this example). The objective of this set is to provide tools that allow the golfer to hit shots relatively consistent distances. For the sake of argument, pick 190 yards for a three iron, 180 for a four iron, followed by a consistent 10-yard gap down to the wedges. The objective is consistency, with each club producing its particular yardage. With all the design variables, there must be one constant to produce the desired results: efficient club head speed at impact. This is the thinking that drove club design for many years, and in sets for elite players it still applies.

Back in 2000 I was laid up recovering from knee surgery. From my back porch I could watch golfers playing a par-three with a carry over water. From three sets of tees I observed the same pattern, as golf balls went to a watery grave. I knew their thinking: "It's 160 yards. That's what I hit with a six iron, so here goes." Some made it, some didn't. As I watched this, a thought crossed my mind: Something is missing in club design; we are doing it wrong.

The next time I visited Adams I passed my thought on to some of the R&D guys. We shouldn't design sets; we should design for shots. In the "set formula," inconsistency was the missing factor. It wasn't just the practice of stronger lofts for weaker players, it was analyzing what head design launches the ball, say, 180 yards in the air given a specific swing speed. Then you design in whatever forgiveness you can to help the human error factor. After you optimize the 180-yard shot, you start over for the 170-yard shot, and so on through the set. You design from the shot desired back to the head, not the other way around. It's a new approach.

I have to stop here and make one thing clear. Most likely I was waking up to something our R&D guys already knew. I have no idea, and I'm certainly not staking any claim to any products that followed. I have lots of conversations with R&D as ideas come and go; fortunately for me, I'm not on a time deadline for a new product release.

The process for creating club design is now completely different than in the relatively recent past, and this benefits golfers of all skill levels. Today's club designs start with an accumulation of data, the source being some type of launch monitor. You can hit balls using machines or humans, indoors or outdoors, and collect data—things like spin, launch angle, and ball speed, and a lot more. You then factor this data into establishing the mass properties of the club being hit, let's say a driver. Does the design you're working with launch the ball high? Low? Is the spin and launch angle what you expect the design to deliver? This is critical; note that I didn't ask if the results were optimal, because they never are. They may be optimal relative to your objectives, but as you learn you increase your database. A good R&D department constantly updates its database. You don't start new designs from scratch; you set new goals based on previous efforts.

So we collect this data, and the combination of testing and design tells us that the driver head is of a certain size with the weight specifically located. Let's stop here before we rush off. What does the head look like?

The formula works roughly like this: "the stranger the design, the better it must perform." A spell of poor shots from a strange-looking club makes it a strong entry for quick placement in the garage. Golfers have enough pressure trying to optimize results with their swings. Now add a funny-looking club and the scale can quickly overload.

Back to R&D. We don't want to commit thousands of dollars to have samples made without a good visual review, so we turn to our latest technology, a device that makes a full-size plastic replica of our head design and does so in a few hours. It not only produces the head but it does so with a hosel so we can insert a shaft and look at the club in the address position. This is a critical step. Sometimes small changes to optimize weight distribution have a detrimental effect on the look of a club, and this process provides a format for optimizing both.

Now we have a head that looks good and plays as designed. It's time to get initial samples for field-testing. What used to be a time-consuming process is now reduced to a computer uploading design files to your manufacturing source, most likely in mainland China. Add in a few weeks for scheduling, and you have samples to hit.

This is an example of the tremendous increase in the sophistication involved in manufacturing heads. Years ago the heads would be cast in the United States, but the finishing costs were very high, so heads were sent to Taiwan, and in some cases Mexico, for mass-production. The Taiwanese, being very industrious, incorporated the forming process so you had one-stop shopping with them. They also did most of the work for the Japanese market, and over time ran into a problem. There was too much finishing work for their available labor, which was getting more costly on an annual basis, so they took the short trip to China.

There they invested in manufacturing facilities, supplying funding and technology while utilizing China's cheap labor supply. Back in the early days when Callaway popularized the use of titanium in driver heads, the only manufacturing sources were in the U.S. Today, some twenty years later, they're almost all in China, and it isn't just the use of materials. The Chinese have also developed very sophisticated processes for blending different materials, which gives the designer flexibility to optimize mass properties.

It's easy to see the "chicken/egg" situation. Do we start out to design a multiple-material driver head, or does our study requiring specific weight distribution cause us to use different materials? Was the spring effect in the face the original design, or did it happen as we made faces thinner and thinner so we could redistribute the weight elsewhere? My honest answer is that I don't know but, for those who read history, I can at least identify sources that could have been the inspiration. I'm not for a minute implying that current club designs were lifted from historic efforts (although maybe a few were); They dealt with different head and shaft weights, differently performing golf balls, and different course conditions. I find the thought processes and materials used hundreds of years ago fascinating, but on further review they shouldn't be that different from what we have today. The objective in club design hasn't changed since the very first effort. It's A+F—airborne and forward. If that seems too simplistic, let me explain.

In any era of golf the objective has been to strike a ball lying on the ground (or tee) and move it forward. Whatever the distance, whatever the conditions, the objective hasn't changed. If you don't get the ball airborne it's pretty hard to move it forward. Anyone who has worked a range, whether teaching or club-fitting, understands this with great clarity. Some examples follow. They do not necessarily represent the earliest designs, but they certainly show the thought processes used by designers long ago. When I peruse *The Clubmaker's Art,* I get two feelings: "That looks familiar," and "WOW, with a bit of upgrading that has some potential." In no particular order I offer the following.

A brief historical review:
1) Hybrids: I talk about these elsewhere because I feel they represent one of the most significant advances to golfers of all skill levels I've seen in thirty years. In the late 1500s there was a set of clubs called the Troon clubs, three to four woods and five or six irons in a set, the shape of the long-nose woods looking more like today's long iron hybrid than a pure wood design. The minute I turned to page twenty-five in *The Clubmaker's Art,* I laughed. Our newest designs certainly resemble a twenty-first-century version of a more than four-hundred-year-old set of clubs. I've had the chance to hit some of these classic designs. Thank heaven for modern materials and optimized mass properties.
2) Multiple Material Usage: Take, for example, the Forgan middle spoon from 1863. Incidentally, Forgan introduced the Bulger Brassey in 1888. It was the first wood club to feature face bulge. I've never seen this innovation referenced, yet it changed the way woods (metals) are designed to this day. In 1919, Waverly Horton introduced a multiple-material wood that is nicely perimeter-weighted.
3) Low Profile Woods: too many to mention from the original Troon set onward. In reading, one thing I found interesting was that the early designers used the size of the golf balls to

influence the face height of their clubs. This is exactly what I did with the Tight Lies club.

4) Anti-shank Wedges: These are clubs with the face forward of the shaft: George Lowe's patent for exactly that design was granted in 1896, but he was preceded by (among others) Francis A. Farlie in 1891. I'm so happy to know shanks go back more than a hundred years.

5) Offset Drivers: Alex N. Weir successfully sold very nice-looking offset woods in the early 1900s.

6) Sand Wedge: Well, all of us amateur historians know that Gene Sarazen invented the sand wedge—except for the fact that he didn't. Mr. Edwin MacClain of Houston, Texas, received a U.S. patent on a sand wedge in 1928, its unique design featuring a large sole with a deep flange. This club was used by Bobby Jones to escape from the sand and birdie the par-five sixteenth while competing in (and winning) the 1930 British Open. The design also featured a concave face found to be illegal by the USGA in their 1931 meeting. It wasn't the sole, but the concave face they objected to, as they determined grassy lies could produce double hits. The sand wedge continued on but with a straight face. Sarazen did come up with a very popular version in 1933, and if you look closely at that model it bears a very strong resemblance to the popular R 90 sand wedges sold today.

7) Metal woods: In the 1890s there were dozens of designs using a variety of metals. The first patent for a metal wood was awarded to William Currie Jr. in 1891.

8) Spring Effect: Sorry. A patent was given to Edward Slade in 1896 for his "spring face wood."

9) Adjustable Weight Woods: Start with Horace Kent and his patent for a weight-adjustable wood granted in 1917.

10) Launch Monitor: I could give dozens of other examples of club designs, teaching aids, and custom-fitting clubs, but I

have to mention my favorite. One of the great advances in club design today is the launch monitor, the ability to hit shots and collect data. In 1921 Mr. Charles Leven patented his practice driver, a club with a built-in mechanism that recorded performance. Now, this wasn't a launch monitor, but take the idea of collecting data at the moment of impact, apply today's technology, and it isn't the greatest stretch to fuse the two.

11) Square Headed Drivers: Horace Hutchison patented his design in 1892. His claims included better alignment and the ability to optimize weight, especially toward the toe for more solid hits.

The square head is a perfect example of then and now. Today's designs are very complex. They were not even possible until manufacturing processes combined the mixing of certain materials, which is very recent technology. Yet, back in 1892, Mr. Hutchinson, a two-time British Amateur winner, was talking about optimum weight disposition. I wonder if he used the term MOI? (MOI means moment of inertia in the head. The higher the MOI, the less deflection on off-center hits.)

Karsten Solheim, founder of PING, is generally credited with introducing perimeter weighting to club head design, most specifically in his Ping Eye irons. In fact, he wasn't the first. In 1905 Arthur Tooley patented his "straight driving iron" with visible heel/toe weighting. In 1932 James Hunt received a patent involving a cavity back perimeter-weighted iron. I don't mean to denigrate anything attributed to Mr. Solheim, because his was a major contribution. He brought us unique perimeter-weighted clubs that were investment cast, as opposed to the forging process used at the time. Being a pioneer, he was ridiculed. People said that his clubs had no feel, that they looked ugly. But as time went on, good shots made his clubs feel better and look better. Today investment casting is the manufacturing method used for most iron heads. Without it and the ensuing process improvements, today's iron head technology would be impossible, and we have Karsten Solheim to thank for it.

Gary Adams (no relation), founder of TaylorMade Golf in 1979, is credited with updating the design and manufacturing technology involved in making "wood" heads out of metal, which effectively ended the persimmon era. It also did one other thing, which was probably more dramatic. It opened the door for a variety of golf ball designs. Previously the solid range balls used were like rockets off irons but destroyed persimmon-headed woods. As metal woods became the norm, golf ball designers entered into a new era of formulation for performance.

The Callaway company took metal wood technology to another level with the introduction of titanium heads that were oversized and had no hosel. Once again, the ideas of oversized heads and no hosel date back to the turn of the century, but titanium was a new material. Like Karsten Solheim's, early Callaway efforts were ridiculed by the establishment. They were ugly and sounded terrible at impact, but again superior performance dispelled these criticisms. All top-of-the-line drivers today are made either from titanium or titanium and a mix of other materials.

I consider these three examples to be the most significant golf head improvements in my thirty years' experience. I am not ignoring shafts. The most significant change was from wood to steel, which happened in the 1920s with steel first being sanctioned for tournament play in 1929. The wood shafts were relatively light, inconsistent, and very flexible, whereas the first steel shafts were relatively heavy, very stiff, and as a result very consistent. The emergence of steel shafts caused elite golfers to adjust their swings accordingly. It has been written that this change influenced the early retirement of Bobby Jones, the great amateur who did not like the new material.

There are two important questions regarding design. Why is it so complex? And aren't we running out of ideas? I use this visual for my answer. Pretend you're at a crowded driving range. Now elevate yourself so you can float above everyone and look down at their swings. What an amazing assembly of physical contortions, yet they all have the exact same goal: they are trying to hit the ball with the club face square at the correct arc of their swing.

Given the endless variety of swings involved, I'd say the designers have significant challenges that will last several years. Add in the fact that ruling bodies limit what they are allowed to provide and it becomes apparent that survival in the field of equipment design will be achieved by only the very skillful.

THIRTY

PGA SHOW DEATHS

*T*he PGA Merchandise Show, held annually around the end of January in Orlando, Florida, was at one time the biggest, most important event in the industry and to a lesser degree still is. An international show, exhibitors come from all over the world and man booths to display products sold into the world of golf. There's everything from clubs to clothing, tournament prizes, vacation spots, and anything else you can think of associated with golf.

Fully half the show is dedicated to equipment—clubs and putters. The attendees are not the general public, but golf professionals, retail owners, buyers, and international distributors. The show was historically big and costly to attend, but if you had plans to sell your products on a grand scale, attendance was mandatory.

The PGA show is where Ely Callaway, Karsten Solheim, and Gary Adams first displayed their wares and answered questions.

Hallowed ground for an equipment guy. I remember my own time there over a span of some thirty years, and despite years of desperation my thoughts are fond. The show has changed today. Some of the top-tier companies no longer attend, and those that do are scaled back from the glory days. In a way, this is an advantage for a small company with an innovative product. Influential buyers still attend and, if some of the big guys don't, that gives you a better shot at recognition.

During its glory years the show itself became an event more dramatic than the products on display. Booths were bigger than my small manufacturing company's offices; sound systems were so powerful you couldn't hold a conversation next door so, to get even, neighbors cranked up their own systems. Famous players and celebrities were in regular attendance. Was it out of control? In retrospect, certainly. But at the time it was the event of the year on our side of the business.

Over the years I've been contacted by people who wanted to enter the golf equipment business. They had already decided to make the commitment, and viewed me as a resource that could facilitate the process. If I'd leveled with them, the conversations would have been less than pleasant, and certainly not what they wanted to hear. In this chapter I am putting you, the reader, into the role of someone who is desirous of entering the business. It represents the dream of many golfers and makes the subject easier to discuss.

Let's say I have invited you to have lunch at my club, where we can have a long discussion under comfortable circumstances. I ask that you ignore the hostile stares and grumbling emanating from the large table in the back. These are the guys I normally play with, and seeing me with a guest means a loss of sure income. It's very unsettling to them. I realize that attending the PGA show as a supplier is part of your dream, so I have conducted some research and will start using the results as a basis for my presentation.

Recently, I reviewed show programs from the years 1990 to 2000. I chose these specific years for two reasons: 1) the equipment business was relatively strong in that period, at least up to the Callaway announcement of 1998; and 2) around 2000 to 2001, many of the major equipment companies stopped attending, and I wanted to reference a period of show and industry strength. One statistic jumped out at me, something I cannot avoid discussing.

In Memoriam:

Accuform Golf, Accurad Golf, Address Golf, Advanced Stag Golf Products, Aim, Alien Golf, All American Golf, Allied Golf, Armour, Atrigon Golf, Avid Golf, Barber Golden Touch, Beauwood, Bel Air Golf, Bert Dargie Golf, Bird Golf, Black Ice, Black Rock Golf, Brann Custom Golf, Browning, Cactus Golf, Carbite, Cayman Golf, Chicago Golf, Compass Golf, Con Sole Golf, Confidence, Coors Cerasports, Crane Golf, Cubic Balance, Custom Craft Golf, Delta Golf, Diawa, Dint USA, Dunlop Golf Clubs, Dura Golf, Echelon, Feel Golf, Fiber Speed, Fila, Fore Star Golf, Founders Club, Gary Player Golf, Gator Sports, Ginty Golf, Golden Golf, Goldwin Golf, Golf Gear, Grand Golf Design, H&B Powerbilt, Head Golf, Hi Tech Golf, Houma, Hurricane Sports, If, Kenneth Smith, Javelin Blue, Jazz Golf, Joe Powell Golf, Langert Golf, Lion Golf, Liquidmetal, Longball Sports, Lynx Golf, Magique Golf, Manmouth, Maruman Golf, Merit Golf, Mitsushiba Golf, Natural Golf, Northwestern Golf, Ocean Club, Orlimar, Otey Crisman Golf, Pal Joey, Palm Springs Golf, Players Golf, Porsche Design, Positive Putter, PRGR, Pro Group (Arnold Palmer), Pure Golf, Ram, Rawlings, Ray Cook, Reid Lockhart, Slazenger, Slotline, Snake Eyes, Solo, Sounder, Spalding (Hogan), Square Two, Stan Thompson, Tad Moore, Teardrop, Ted Sheftic Custom Clubs, Toney Penna, Roby-Toski, Tour Precision, Traxx, Triumph Golf, Truex Golf Wood Brothers, Yamaha, Zevo, ZT Golf.

Every one of the exhibitors listed above came to the show as a stand-alone company with plans to succeed on a national scale. Today, none of them are significant factors in the market and the vast majority of them are gone. Needless to say, this is a tough business.

Using the word "death" may be a bit theatrical, but to quote a Mickey Newbury song, "The Future's Not What It Used To Be." Some brands in financial distress sold to other operators, such as when Golfsmith bought Lynx and Snake Eyes. Spalding and their subsidiary, Hogan, sold to Callaway, Dunlop to TaylorMade. International companies like Diawa or Houmna chose to exit the U.S. market. Others on the list may still operate on a small regional basis or sell on the Internet. It really doesn't make any difference. This list is partial; it represents hundreds of millions of dollars lost. And these were the *good* years.

Further, I knew many of these companies and their people. They represented excellent, innovative product designs, and had good engineers, PhDs on board, and strong financial backing. They had aggressive marketing, experienced management, infomercials, and so on. Sure, some were financially strapped. Some had no business even going to the show. But look at the numbers. You can't tell me there isn't a message here.

To help explain why so many of these companies failed, let's discuss the metrics of the golf equipment industry as a whole. To start, the market hasn't grown by any significant degree in several years. This data is public information. The industry is also regulated, so any new products must pass a review to be sure they conform to rules, guidelines that go back fifty years or more. This review is conducted by the USGA (United States Golf Association) and their European counterpart, the R&A (Royal and Ancient). (I don't know if the word "counterpart" offends the R&A, as their organization is the home of golf at its origin. I'm just describing two organizations that work together to protect the game.)

What are these organizations working to protect, specifically? History. One of the best aspects of golf is that you can walk fairways in the footsteps of great names from earlier centuries. The USGA and R&A want to protect that history, not forcing you to play with clubs designed in the 1700s, but neither allowing you to use equipment so sophisticated that human skill becomes a minor factor.

There is a natural conflict here. Equipment manufacturers must reinvent or die, a natural effect of a flat market. They do so against published specifications, some of which are open to interpretation by the governing bodies. Each new product is submitted to the ruling bodies and, upon acceptance, is designated as conforming to their rules.

Over the years companies have openly marketed clubs that do not conform which, from a marketing position, is totally legal. The results from that effort are minimal sales, even when a brand as strong as Callaway tried it with their ERC driver. Golfers, by and large, are an honorable group and want to play within the rules.

Say, for example, you make a driver using a new material called sleazium, which comes from a secret source in a distant land. The nature of this material in a driver adds twenty yards in distance to comparable products on the market. The USGA tests your club and, son-of-a-gun, it does add twenty yards. They have no rules on sleazium. It's a new material, so you plan to rush to market. Unfortunately, you get a notice that your driver is ruled nonconforming. How can this happen? Along with all the published specifications, the ruling bodies have the power to make decisions "for the good of the game," and under that aegis your club fails. Adding that much distance off the tee would surely make some courses obsolete, and it would be because of the driver's material, not a golfer's swing. You can run newspaper ads saying, "Breakthrough sleazium material drives golf balls too far." It's a small market, generally centered in Atlantic City and Las Vegas.

The fact is that, given the lack of growth in the population of players and the high number of equipment companies, there is too much product in the market. Every sale you make will be to a potential customer of large, well-established companies. They have more than twenty years' head start in product usage and brand awareness. Raw material costs are increasing, but ultimate prices are decreasing, causing a margin squeeze.

Nevertheless, new companies enter the market every year propelled by passion and with a faith that they can overcome all of the many obstacles standing in their way. It is relatively inexpensive to develop product for the golf industry. But marketing costs will run you into the tens of millions very quickly, and it will be years before they develop a significant return. Of course, during all this time your competitors aren't waiting for you to catch up. They have far greater resources for product development and marketing and, I assure you, are working as hard and effectively as they know how to hold their market positions.

If you find the data presented so far discouraging, I don't blame you. It's a very, very competitive business, and it takes more than a great product and significant luck to survive. If you don't believe me, take a second look at the list above.

THIRTY-ONE

THE GOLF EQUIPMENT INDUSTRY

*A*llow me to turn back the clock and give you a bit of history. If you want to compete in today's market, understanding how it evolved is worth the effort.

Back at the turn of the century, the Scots exported golf professionals to the United States. These were teachers, club designers and builders, custom-fitters, and often course designers. They would watch you swing and then sand a piece of hickory to attach to a club head, the objective being a completed club for your particular game. I can hear the conversation, "Aye, Tom, ye making shafts for Mr. Bigblurb?" "Sure enough, Arch, with tha lunge he makes it will take more than a wee bit of work on some hickory." Some things never change, just the times.

As golf became more popular, this laborious process gave way to mass-produced products. One of the first companies in the business was A. G. Spalding. Wood shafts then gave way to steel. Thanks to Walter Hagen, golf professionals were actually allowed to enter the clubhouse, and shortly thereafter a professional playing tour was started.

The game grew slowly and steadily, and in time great players like Byron Nelson, Ben Hogan, Sam Snead, and Bobby Jones emerged. Soon, certain tournaments took on significant prestige such as the Masters, the U.S. Open, and the PGA championship. The granddaddy of them all was the British Open, or "the Open," as referenced by the good folks in the UK.

I know that this is ancient history oft written about elsewhere, but in my own fashion I'm making a point. The stars had to align for the game to take a popular leap forward, and eventually they did. The ingredients were Arnold Palmer and television. If you watch old film of televised golf you'll notice that it was an evolving technology struggling to show the complexity of the game and the great skills of the players. Somehow Arnie superseded all the televising difficulties, and viewing audiences loved him. TV golf prospered, and the game grew in popularity.

As the game prospered, more people played and more companies entered the equipment industry. Some already present were grand old sporting goods names like Wilson, Rawlings, and H&B Powerbilt. Great players had company associations, names including Hogan, Palmer, Player, Nicklaus, and Tommy Armour. I mention all these for one main reason: None is a top tier company in sales anymore, not even close. Yes, some are still with us and some have new management working very hard. My point is that you would have loved to achieve the brand awareness and market share any of these companies once enjoyed, yet today none is a serious factor in the market.

These were all mature companies with sales forces, marketing programs, customer relations—all the things you don't have. So how do you avoid the same fate? Let's look at the top companies today and see if we can find any clues.

Callaway, TaylorMade, Ping, Cobra, Cleveland, and Titleist are today considered the top-tier companies in the golf equipment industry. This is determined by their total sales and market share as determined by independent audit. Some smaller companies have successful niches, but these are the big guys that you'd love to emulate. To put this in clearer perspective, Adams Golf is often referred to as a second-tier company, with annual sales nearing $100 million on just golf clubs.

It's important I reemphasize something I mentioned earlier: Golf equipment in general is and essentially has been a flat market for the past several years. I know the stories about maturing baby boomers and their disposable income, and when you look at the world market an argument can be made that it is actually down. I'm not going into all the reasons why. Suffice it to say that there is good data available to support this position and I can provide dozens of articles from within the industry on the challenge of getting more people to play golf.

What it means to everyone attempting to sell golf equipment is that your competition is essentially those top tier companies, and every club you sell is one less that they would have sold. Don't tell me you're too smart to start off competing against these guys. They are exactly your competition.

Let's play a word association game. I'll name the words and you guess what I'm talking about. Wedges, the Baffler, Bullseye, Ping, metal heads, oversized titanium drivers. Yes, it's way too simple; you are an experienced golfer and you associate these products with the companies I've listed in the top tier. Each of these successful companies started with a singular product. That particular product might not have been their first and it certainly wasn't their last, but they focused their time and money marketing one thing, and with success from that expanded their lines. Along the way the older companies with full lines of clubs found themselves losing market

share. They found themselves outside the perception (and sometimes reality) of being innovators.

Start with Titleist, which is historically a golf ball company and
in my opinion the best-managed operation in the industry. Back
in the 1950s they first marketed the Bullseye putter, which they
acquired from a Phoenix golf pro named John Reuters. Cleveland
was known for its wedges and dominated that category for years.
TaylorMade was formed to market one product; "wood" heads made
from metal. Cobra (now owned by Titleist) struggled with full sets,
then became known for its Baffler, a railed fairway wood, before
moving into oversized irons. Ping started with the sound "ping."
One of its first putters, the 1A, had a very thin face that made a
resounding ping sound at impact. They went on to a series of successful heel/toe weighted putters and innovated perimeter-weighted
investment cast irons, but on day one it was the 1A putter.

Finally, there's Callaway. It's good to pay special attention to them
because they changed the golf industry. Ely Callaway was considered
a marketing genius long before he entered the golf business. His background was in the textile industry, which he left in 1973 to start a wine
business. What's the tie-in? Nothing, except of course an excellence in
marketing. His wines were a great success, and in 1981 he sold the
company for $14 million. His next venture was to purchase a small
golf equipment company called Hickory Sticks for $400,000. The
tremendous success story of Callaway Golf has been well chronicled.

But truth be told, it wasn't that easy. Ely had modest success with
the Hickory Sticks, which were wedges with steel shafts coated to
look like wood. They were nice clubs,but nothing extraordinary,
and he was smart enough to sell them in a beautiful wooden display
rack. I remember one club pro telling me that if nothing else, he
bought the wedges to get the display rack (just a little marketing
gem to file away).

While the business grew at a modest rate, it wasn't exciting and
didn't have the potential to keep someone like Ely interested, so

he found a buyer. They agreed on a price but the buyer had one stipulation. He wanted Ely to stick around and run the place for six months to a year. Ely wasn't interested; frankly, he'd had it with the golf equipment industry and told the buyer that the sale didn't include him. The buyer was not an operator, did not have someone else to move into the business, and the sale fell through.

Ely now faced a decision. He could either find another buyer or figure out a way to make the company substantial. One thing he knew for sure: His main competitors, Spalding, Wilson, Powerbilt, *et al*, were working with very old marketing plans. You could call it the "we've always done it that way" school of design and marketing.

There are tons of stories available on the history of Callaway Golf and its successes. I don't need to be their historian here, except as it provides lessons for aspiring members of the equipment industry. Ely returned to his little company with renewed vigor. He brought in designer Dick Helmstetter and they stressed innovation beginning with their hosel-less irons, the S2H2, introduced in 1988.

Fast-forward to 1991 and the introduction of the Big Bertha, a driver that changed the golf industry. When the Bertha came out, it sounded funny. In golf, sound and feel are synonymous, and I was at the PGA Merchandise Show listening to the old guard question the high-pitched sound it made on impact. Further, the club looked different, and finally, it not only used a new material, titanium, but these drivers were priced to sell for $400 which was far above the norm at that time. The established companies fell all over themselves laughing at what they knew was pure folly. As it turned out, the only thing pure was the success. A new sheriff had arrived and he was going to change the game.

Before you get all excited about using Callaway as a success model, there are a few details to bear in mind. In 1991 the old guard still had a strong industry position, conducting business as they had for many years. Callaway looked at the industry in a different vein, though. They weren't just interested in selling product.

Their goal was industry domination. They raised big money, offered tour players new lucrative contracts, used celebrity endorsements outside golf, and made more money for retailers by increasing their margins.

Within a few years (and a public offering), they completely dominated equipment sales. The old guard essentially became the dead guard. Competition came from new, innovative companies that learned from Callaway and figured out how to compete with their model. This is a good place to give TaylorMade credit for their marketing efforts over the last few years. With the power of a large corporate owner, Adidas, they have become a formidable competitor for Callaway and the two are the significant overall market leaders for golf clubs.

If the idea of being recognized as innovative started with a single club years ago, it's mandatory now. A new club-maker's only chance for success today is to focus marketing on one club or one category and to gain a reputation for innovation, because its innovation that drives equipment sales.

In the words of an infomercial, "But wait, there's more." This strategy does not include drivers. They are the focus club for the big companies like Callaway and TaylorMade, and simply stated, you have no chance to compete with them. They invest millions in marketing and advertising. They have huge R&D staffs and a relationship with consumers and retailers. Remember, equipment is regulated and the USGA is particularly concerned about controlling distance, so no matter how good your driver is it comes down to marketing, a game you cannot win. Looking at the history of the last twenty years; concentrating on other clubs in the bag has produced some success, but TaylorMade and Callaway thoroughly dominated driver sales.

This is as good a time as any to give you a deeper bit of insight into survival in the equipment business. I mentioned the ruling bodies and their specifications, especially regarding drivers and hitting the ball farther. One of the magnificent things about golf as played at the highest level is that the players police themselves. They will see an infraction (say, a minuscule movement of the golf ball that no one else sees), stop play, contact an official, and assess themselves the appropriate penalty. It's one of the greatest honor codes in all of sport.

But let's say a major equipment company finds out that one of their drivers, already on retail shelves, exceeds one of the specifications controlling distance. Do they immediately notify the USGA, point out the problem, and accept the response? That would result in a public identification of the offending product and normally the company, through its distribution, would be forced to trade consumers for conforming versions. This tends to have a negative effect on the brand, not surprisingly, and could drive consumers elsewhere.

In the above instance the legitimate companies encountering a problem like this will do their best to weed out nonconforming product, conduct business as usual, and work with their suppliers to preclude future problems. They run their operations to produce product within spec, and such instances are rare. At the same time, drivers are about distance, and every company knows they walk a very fine line.

Policing would be easy if the USGA and other ruling bodies would strategically place inspection centers around the golfing world. There, skilled technicians could randomly sample product to ensure adherence to published specs, not just among tour players but for everyday golfers as well. Unfortunately, no such inspection centers exist, and that's why every major company tests their clubs as well as those of their competition. In the uber-competitive world of equipment sales, we have, shall we say, full disclosure.

This isn't a very gentlemanly analysis. If Company A finds a driver from Company B that is out of spec (a competitive advantage of as little as two or three yards on a 260-yard drive), A will rat out B. Samples of B will show up on the doorstep of the ruling body with a note saying "measure the COR" attached. (COR refers to the "spring effect" in the face, which is regulated.)

The plot thickens. B now is involved in a very public trading of their nonconforming model. Do they rest or do they earnestly check the competitor's drivers, especially if they smell the rat? Do more samples with notes attached begin arriving in the dead of night? Do more announcements of nonconforming clubs occur?

Ah, the world of intense competition. I won't even begin to talk about the patent filings and the lovely games that are constantly playing behind the scenes. Far be from me to write about such goings on; after all, I'm retired and don't have firsthand knowledge. But if you'd care to wager . . .

Since a marketing strategy is to have clubs played on the PGA Tour, the process is worth a little discussion. Starting with junior golf, good players are watched by equipment companies who have representatives at that level. They provide free equipment, get to know the parents, and start a relationship. This continues through the levels of play until the person turns professional. At that moment the company can provide money, but it's much more complex. Suppose it's an elite junior who has a teacher (or coach or any influential advisor). A company which plans to sign the junior in the future will try to have that teacher under contract, whether they are providing just clubs or financial compensation. If you're an elite player getting ready to play at the highest level, you're not going to abandon the equipment you've been successful with just because a competing company offers more. Given the tremendous purses available, it makes no sense not to be 100 percent comfortable with one's clubs.

It's different on the minor tours, but even there some players have lucrative contracts based on their potential. However, lots of these professionals are struggling financially and are more receptive to equipment deals. The problem is that except for the Nationwide

Tour there is little or no TV coverage, and companies pay these guys for one thing—TV exposure.

It works like this. Every Thursday at the beginning of a professional tournament, a group from a company called the Darrell Survey looks in each player's bag and carefully notes the brand of each club. They actually lift the head covers, as in the past there were occasionally some brand Y drivers found under brand X head covers (X being the payee). Club contracts revolve around the Darrell Survey, so there have also been clubs put in play on Thursday for the count that are changed for the rest of the tournament. The objective for a company is to dominate a category (such as drivers) and advertise their number-one position. There have been instances where the word "tour" has been misused. An ad will appear in a golf magazine proclaiming Brand Z's driver as number one on tour. Upon deeper inspection, generally by the legal department of the real number-one driver, it turns out that the "tour" in reference is the applesauce tour played in North Dakota in November.

It's understood that we amateurs are influenced by usage on tour. But the clubs the pros are playing are tweaked, even custom-designed for them; after all, they really do play a different game. Consumers pretty much understand that being played on tour means the company is very competent, but might not necessarily buy the specific clubs in play.

That's how it works. The costs, of course, are relative to the visibility of the player, which translates to TV time. One important factor is the player's hat; if your company's name is not on the front, you are missing most of the TV exposure. If you sign player X and get your name on his bag, it's slightly better than an underwear contract. Just watch an event on TV and see what is by far the most visible. Do you pay more for hat presence? Of course.

Remember, this is about the business of professional golf, and that means money. If you decide to get yourself a tour player, it will be low six figures for someone in the top one hundred, and up to seven figures for a top-twenty player. Just getting a couple of top-hundred players is pretty much a waste, unless one of them gets hot and contends in a major tournament. They don't even have to win, just contend. And why, you might ask? I already answered; television exposure.

Signing them is only part of the expense; you also have to employ tour representatives who attend events just to make sure your players are happy. One thing about professional golfers is that whenever something goes wrong, it is not their fault. It's everything from noises to cameras, caddie mistakes, and out-of-adjustment clubs. It's always an external source that caused the poor round or bad shot. You may think that's crazy, but these guys live in a competitive environment of extreme pressure. They have no teammates. It's all on them, and they must maintain their confidence. Part of that is their unwavering belief that they don't hit bad shots—outside influences do. Your representative on tour must have the player's confidence, because I guarantee the competition is somehow getting him the word that maybe it's the clubs.

Finally, there is no sense having players on tour if you don't tell the world, so be prepared to have a significant advertising budget to remind everyone. Do not expect one of your tour players to freely announce that his (your) clubs are the greatest things since ice cream, especially when interviewed after a good round. Why not? Because TV *sells* advertising time. It does not give it away, and therefore such efforts are frowned upon.

Every person I talk to who is either considering entering the golf equipment business or who just loves the game talks about the PGA Tour. That's understandable. The tour boasts the best players in the world, wonderful venues, and coverage from every source of media. Sometimes what gets lost is that it's a business; you don't employ a tour player unless you have a corresponding plan of how it's going to help your business, and even then you may not succeed. An example of a good way to market from tour usage is what a company called Sonartec did with fairway woods a few years ago. Players liked them, they got in some bags, the media picked up on the success, and consumers responded.

Once the big guys figured that out, the screws tightened and Sonartec's presence dropped. Sonartec didn't have the millions of marketing and advertising dollars it took to take advantage of their position, and the company (recently sold) now struggles along with everyone else of their size. They had a good product, but for the umpteenth time: this is a highly competitive business and that fact controls everything. Enough about the tour. I just wanted you to understand that "getting a tour player" is a gross over simplification.

Here's another reality. By the time you attend the January 2009 PGA Merchandise Show, the product line you're developing now will essentially be obsolete! Your competitors have been using their huge distribution systems to show customers the '09 lines starting four months before the show, and for the most part have booked orders for at least the first quarter. The cycle is such that they are now testing product to be shown the following season.

So while going to the show represents a nice, expensive, and basically unproductive experience, you must attend to get an understanding, a feel for how the industry really works. Unfortunately there is no price break for first-time attendees. I know it's crazy, but equipment life cycles in the industry are approximately one year. By the time you have enough brand name, distribution capability, and R&D to compete in that cycle you will have spent years and many, many millions of dollars. Thank the good folks at Callaway for that, because short life cycles were a competitive reaction to their success and are now the norm.

I can think of only two approaches that a smaller equipment company can take that have ever achieved a degree of market penetration. The first, as I demonstrated personally, is through an infomercial. What I didn't mention in the earlier chapters, however, is that the key to any infomercial is that you have to be able to sell your product for a minimum of eight times the cost. Forget the nice product, the innovation; those are givens.

If the retail price is up around $200 or more, you might get away with six times the cost if the infomercial is really successful, but eight times works much better, as do nine and ten times. Eight times the cost is the starting point, and without it I don't care how catchy the infomercial is, you'll just lose money faster. Assuming you have the correct ratio, you must carefully define your objective. One goal might be to sell a single product on the air and create retail demand. If you want to use the infomercial as a springboard to competing in the golf equipment business then you must consider all the competitive situations I discussed earlier. Alien (wedges) and Orlimar (fairway woods) are examples of extraordinarily successful infomercials that could not make the transition to successful operating companies, and the attempt was painfully expensive.

For a real success, look to the two-ball putter from Odyssey. Initially they were part of the Tommy Armour organization, and then sold to Callaway. They sold putters with inserts and did okay, but the success was nothing spectacular. Along came a new design, actually a version of an old Dave Pelz putter with two simulated golf balls behind the face which served as an alignment guide. Tour players used it and it worked well. It was visible on TV and the company had the resources to market and sell their opportunity. It was a huge success because they had all the necessary pieces of the puzzle in place.

The question then is, could you become an Odyssey? Suppose your designer has an idea for a great putter that works and is visible on TV. You would have a chance, but as I sit here I can think of four small innovative putter companies that fit that exact description, and all struggle financially. Why? Because they compete with top-tier companies, which also have innovative putters and fully developed infrastructures for support. This scenario offers a glimmer of hope.

Underline glimmer.

THIRTY-TWO

YOU AND YOUR CLUBS, AN EQUIPMENT QUIZ

/ had a little fun with my industry analysis, but grant me that while it was an effort to keep things interesting, the essence of the story is true. If it discourages a reader from entering the golf equipment business, that was not necessarily the intent. I'll give the Barney version of a great historical statement, "Those who don't study history are subject to lose their shirts."

This chapter is about you and your golf clubs, a quiz from my days at PGA seminars. Given golfers' passion about their equipment, I promise that it will be conducted with appropriate seriousness.

Before I start the quiz, let me give an analysis of a set of clubs as they are sold today. In "my time," we had sets of clubs. They consisted of a driver, two fairway woods, and irons—generally two and three through a sand wedge. It was normal that, with an exception or two, all the clubs would be from the same manufacturer—a matched set. This system has since given way to a combination of application-specific woods and irons. Start with the drivers. They have very large heads, very high momentum, and long, light shafts. They are essentially a specialty club, designed to hit the long bomb with a mostly straight ball flight. They are not ideal for curving the ball or hitting shots off the ground, hence the designation as a specialty club.

Fairway woods are essentially two different categories—three woods and the rest. The three wood of today now embodies the specs of drivers in past years. They range in length from 43 inches down, with lofts as low as 9 or 10 degrees depending on head design. No wonder the pros hit them so far. If I remember correctly, Jack Nicklaus's driver was 42.5 inches long with 11 degrees of loft. The three wood is designed to be hit off a tee and off the ground with a trajectory applicable for the player involved. Subsequent fairway woods are simply players' choice.

Next come the long irons which are now, in many cases, hybrids. Why hybrids? There are several influences. The era of strong lofted clubs in the shorter irons has decreased the group of two, three, and four irons to a narrow loft range that is very difficult to manufacture accurately. These clubs have always been difficult to hit, and the stronger face loft hasn't helped. Fairways are cut tighter than in years past, resulting in tight lies (I love that term) and adding to the difficulty.

Driver and ball design have also affected long irons. I'm serious. Manufacturers know that drivers that hit farther sell more. Decreasing spin while keeping the launch angle is the objective. The same is true for golf balls in an era of softer, lower spin rate balls. Standing over a two or three iron, we need spin to lift the ball or we need significant club head speed to help. Hybrids have a low and rearward center of gravity in their head design, and as a result launch the ball higher with less spin. In other words, for most of us they go farther and that is a good thing. The category of hybrids has been a very interesting development. Tour players embraced them before the general public did. The best players in the world were using hybrids that are more forgiving and easier to hit, especially on high, soft shots. For a long time, amateurs stuck to their long irons, a phenomenon that baffled manufacturers and tour players alike. This has changed now, but it was an interesting period.

Now we get to the iron-looking clubs and, with the knowledge learned from the increased efficiency in the hybrids, manufacturers are providing us with irons that are longer, stronger and easier to hit. Take two competing eight irons, and the one that goes farther sells 90 percent of the time. Trust me, manufacturers know this.

On to wedges, which have become a category of their own. In the old days we carried a pitching wedge and sand wedge. The super-strong lofts created gaps, so a G wedge was introduced. Now we have 60- and 64-degree wedges with different bounces for different head designs. It's important to be aware of the type of course you play and the wedge design you use. You want less bounce for very tight, firm fairways and more bounce (or a wider sole) on your sand wedge for soft fluffy sand. I also suggest that, for 90 percent of amateur players, all wedges with over a 56-degree (standard sand wedge) face loft be given to someone you want to beat. Yes, I am aware of all the advertising copy, but there is one thing missing; practice. It takes some serious practice to develop the feel and technique for these highly lofted clubs; most ranges don't have an adequate area. Even if they do, I guarantee the time spent hitting drivers compared to wedges is 10:1. The mis-hit 60-or 64-degree wedge almost always leads to a disaster, like getting buried in a trap or getting skulled over the green into a spot where mortals fear to venture.

Now that I've given you the big picture on clubs, lets get to some specifics in a manner that is both fun and interesting. The approach is one I've used in the past, a simple true-or-false quiz. The questions that follow are selected from some thirty-five I've used over the years, and the objective here is to give you information that will help you select the best equipment for your own game. Let me start with one basic suggestion: Whenever possible, hit clubs before you purchase them. If the season doesn't allow, go indoors. The new sensor technology for hitting balls indoors is outstanding, and you can get great feedback.

The reason I recommend this approach is the human factor. I have custom-fit as many clubs as most in the business, and one thing I know is that whenever I think I can watch someone make a couple of swings and call out their specs, I'll be wrong. With that, I hope what follows is helpful.

1) The heart and soul of any golf club is the shaft.
   True _____ **False** _____

2) Longer-shafted drivers produce more distance.
   True _____ **False** _____

3) If you buy a five wood and hit it great, buy a three wood with the same specs to get even more distance.
   True _____ **False** _____

4) Since graphite shafts are lighter you will swing the club faster, producing more distance.
   True _____ **False** _____

5) Forged heads produce a softer feel at impact.
   True _____ **False** _____

6) If a new club doesn't look playable at address, don't worry; it will improve over time.
   True _____ **False** _____

7) You can get clubs made from non-brand components that will perform as well as the expensive brands.
   True _____ **False** _____

8) It's an industry secret that companies use inexpensive graphite shafts in their woods to save money.
   True _____ **False** _____

9) Graphite shafts fatigue over time, especially if exposed to serious heat or cold.
   True _____ **False** _____

10) The longest tee shots are those bullets that go in a straight line and roll forever.
    True _____ **False** _____

11) Softer shafts and softer golf balls work best for most golfers.
    True _____ **False** _____

12) Custom fit clubs will cause you to swing better.
    True _____ **False** _____

13) This last question is a multiple choice: You enter a golf shop where the professional has been granted magic powers. He can grant you one golf wish. You get to improve your game, and make it more like that of a tour player. There are four choices: A) longer, straighter tee shots; B) longer, accurate second shots, say, from 160 yards to more than 200; C) more accurate short shots including wedges and chipping; or D) better putting. Whatever the degree of improvement, it will be the same in each category, so to move your game closer to that of the touring professional, you get to pick one, which will produce the best result. You, in this case, are an avid golfer, say a bit better than average, a sixteen handicap. **A** _____ **B** _____ **C** _____ **D** _____

The Answers

These answers are relative to a majority of golfers. As a fitter, I came across exceptions to just about everything, so don't contact me about your Uncle Mycroft who plays the opposite of every answer, as I've already met him.

(1) *The heart and soul of any golf club is the shaft.* FALSE. Furthermore, the shaft can be considered the most overrated part of a golf club!

If this one doesn't get your attention, you should put the book down because 99 percent of the honest reactions are TRUE. Furthermore, my answer is often met with skepticism (at best). Before I go into detail, let me remind you that I have access to some of the best shaft experts in the golf industry and am pretty careful when I discuss controversial subjects.

Let's start with history. I'll recite from Barney's list of equipment blunders, in this case the J driver. Approximately twenty years ago, Jumbo Ozaki, the great Japanese player, arrived to play in the Masters with a Bridgestone driver named after him, called the J driver. Among other pros, Greg Norman used one, and throughout the tournament the announcers talked about this club and the incredible distances it produced. It was the kind of TV response every equipment manufacturer dreams of, and the club became a phenomenon. Way before Callaway, the J driver had an oversized head and was expensive by the standards of the time, and golfers had to have one.

There were sign-up lists at stores and pro shops. Golfers with access traveled to Japan and returned with as many as they could find. Some sold them for enough to finance the trip plus make a significant profit.

This product should have influenced golf equipment for years to come, but it didn't. It had one rather minor flaw: in the hands of the average golfing public, it was almost unhittable. The ball went low and right, not a desired ball flight for a driver. What did the smart golfers do? They had it reshafted, some more than once, but the results were essentially the same. The club was acceptable to some elite players, but there was no market for the average golfer, and people had bought it with the most positive expectations.

Back around 1970, I remember that a fellow golf nut showed up with a radical new set of irons he'd bought, called Ping. By the standards of the time ugly they were, and received great ridicule. Their inventor, Karsten Solheim, was not easily deterred, believing that he had a superior product design. (I bet he had some WOW responses.) Over the years his product was not only accepted, it became the number one-selling iron in the industry (an overnight success after fifteen years), praised by golfers of all skill levels. He enjoyed an iron market share never before achieved by one company. What wasn't universally known at the time was Karsten's choice of shafts. They were X flex, designed not just for strong players, but for everyone! These irons are still in play, loved by their owners, and during my "in shop" days I had a lot of fun showing people what they were actually using. I might add, I also told them that they were (and are) a great club. Shafts overrated? You could certainly say so in this case.

No rational club fitter today would prescribe X flex shafts for all his customers regardless of club head speed. Yet the Ping Eyes did exactly that and received universal praise. I've had people say it was because they used light shafts, but they were only slightly lighter than the standard shafts of the time. The club "played" lighter because the grips were heavier. I know this was back in the '80s, but I don't think the human race was much different then than it is today. The Ping Eyes enjoyed the largest market share in iron sales and was universally praised, yet its shafts were in violation of all known standards for flex.

The J driver was simply a head design that did not work for less than very high swing speeds. If the head design is off, you can't save the club with a shaft. The Ping Eye irons were a bit more complex, but they were very consistent, very well balanced, and had a great head design. The common denominator here is head design. Do the job right and you can optimize performance with a shaft, so the answer can be true in certain instances.

Even then it is a complex area. I fully subscribe to the philosophy that well-designed driver heads for some players can be optimized with a shaft fitting, especially given the electronic analysis available today. This is true for fairway woods and hybrids, but less true as you get into short irons and wedges. Most golfers I've seen could play with a stiff shaft in their wedges with no letdown in performance, even with nine and eight irons. It's quite individual. If some golfers knew they had an S shaft in their wedge, they would have a hard time hitting good shots even if it was correct. Such is the mental aspect of the game.

What exactly is the job of the shaft? To return the club head to the ball in a square position so the maximum energy can be transmitted. The shaft does not create energy. From a playing standpoint you want a shaft that does its job in a repetitive manner, something you feel confident you can use. Let's say you should play an R flex shaft. That doesn't mean you can't muscle up and make solid contact with an S. It just means that the R fits your swing, and using an R you'll be able to perform more consistently. The reason why the answer to this question is false is that a good club is includes a good head, shaft, and grip. And if some component part is off, it cannot be fixed with just the shaft.

(2) *Longer-shafted drivers produce more distance.* TRUE. This has been proven on machine tests and through human testing. The USGA has placed a 48-inch limit on drivers; most of the long-drive contestants use drivers 48 inches and longer.

If the answer is so clear, then why the question? Because the Web is full of columns by golfing experts. I have read various entries that state the optimum length for a driver is 44 inches, 44.5 inches, a variety of lengths, wherein the author of the site purports to have some magic insight (and no test data) into driver length. They claim that any longer than their standard, and your off-center miss-hits increase, negating any value of the long shaft.

That just isn't true, especially in this era of high-MOI heads; it's still an individual game and you may not be comfortable with extra length, but it's worth trying. I'm not saying everyone will hit longer shaft-length drivers for greater distance, as some people just can't adjust to the extra length. I'm saying the potential is there.

(3) *If you buy a five wood and hit it great, buy a three wood with the same specs to get even more distance.* FALSE. This is a very common misconception. Let's say you are assigned the job of watering the lawn, more specifically the flowers at the end of the lawn. You have the hose stretched as far as it will go and the water pressure on full blast. If you hold the hose parallel to the ground the water doesn't reach the flowers; hold it perpendicular and you water yourself. But hold the hose at the proper angle and the water reaches the flowers. The water pressure is club head speed and the hose is launch angle. It very well could be that the five wood is optimum for you to reach the flowers and a three wood will not go as far. This is something you need to test before running out and buying a three wood.

(4) *Since graphite shafts are lighter you will swing the club faster, producing more distance.* FALSE. Well, false in irons and up to about 42 inches in woods. After that, it's true. You can be right with either answer if you were thinking about certain clubs. I have included the question because it's one

I've been asked countless times at demo days. Speed only counts at the moment of impact. I've seen many players hit graphite shorter because they swung the club faster in the backswing but couldn't time their impact properly. I can't tell you how many times I've seen slow-swinging seniors and ladies hit steel shafts farther. I can't tell you how many times, in possession of this hard data, I've heard them say, "Well, I really like graphite." And I say, "Yes, certainly," because I know if they have a mindset that steel doesn't work for them, it won't. Based on years of range experience I see no special value in graphite shafts. The exception is in the minds of golfers, their perception, and that is a major consideration.

Starting with longer clubs, approximately 42 inches, graphite is preferable. The overall length, head weight, and lighter shaft can be engineered to produce more distance. Rarely do you see product on the market that doesn't use graphite for these lengths, and it's just about universal in drivers.

(5) *Forged heads produce a softer feel at impact.* FALSE. Since Adams Golf produces a forged head, I can ramble on without being accused of company-bashing. Forged heads have what is known as a long grain, and they are easy to bend. However, this softness is not the same as impact softness. A soft feel at impact is the absence of vibration, and that comes from club head design.

While I'm discussing feel, let me include a major factor—sound. It's well known among manufacturers that feel and sound are so closely associated as to be often considered one and the same. In tests, consumers have picked out the best-feeling clubs with great certainty, only to wear sound inhibitors and not be able to repeat their conclusions. Nothing is wrong with forging, but there's no magic feel inherent from the process.

(6) *If a new club doesn't look playable at address, don't worry; it will improve over time.* FALSE. It's essential that when looking at a club in the address position, the message to your golfing system must be, "Wow, I can hit this." If the message isn't there, you will lose faith in the clubs long before there is any grudging acceptance.

(7) *You can get clubs made from non-brand components that will perform as well as the expensive brands.* FALSE. Before I get the wrath of the components guys, read my answer and remember I was once a components guy. I see the process that goes into club design: months of research and testing. Designs are refined down to 0.005 of an inch to ensure the exact location of the mass properties. Engineers use different weight materials in the same head, stringent controls, and quality checks to be sure that product is made to specification. I have been in the Asian operations of some of the largest components builders. They may make clubs that externally resemble well-known brands, but the internal design and control of mass properties is not the same. In this case I'm referencing drivers, but the complex design technology runs throughout the set.

The incredible competition in the golf business forces big-brand manufacturers to continually fine-tune their products, and even smaller companies really have to hustle to keep up, much less component houses. "Uncle Mycroft is a beginner, so why should he shell out his hard-earned cash to show off a brand?" You ask. "I know that half that cost is marketing money, not the true cost of the components." I told you I have been to this rodeo. Tell your uncle to look for deeply discounted models from last year; they weren't bad, and this year's improvements aren't quantum leaps better. Use the savings to take lessons.

(8) *It's an industry secret that companies use inexpensive graphite shafts in their woods to save money.* FALSE. Years ago there was

some truth to this, but not today. No chance. Take someone small like Adams: we have twenty-seven R&D personnel (and growing). It takes months to design and test, say, a new driver; over a year is not uncommon. So after all that time and expense, are we going to just throw in a cheap shaft to save money, then go out and compete against the best in the industry? If it's a major brand they have the same issues, only more expense; they are not going to use a cost-saving cheap shaft so someone like us can kick their butt.

Once you design a head, you go into extensive testing to pick a shaft design that helps provide optimum performance. Do you negotiate for the best prices? Certainly, but not by sacrificing quality.

Now you're a shaft company, you've just gone through this process with a major equipment manufacturer, and during the testing you find out that the shaft pattern they like is really pretty good. You can market it under your own name, with a different color pattern and different brand, and sell it for considerably more as a component to the independent shops. Have I ever seen anyone reshaft their driver with what I know is *very* close to the same shaft, color being the big difference? Of course, and they are convinced it's better.

(9)   *Graphite shafts fatigue over time, especially if exposed to serious heat or cold.* FALSE. In the old days this was true, but today's resins are impervious to those types of ambient conditions. As for steel shafts, they may start to fatigue after about fifty years.

(10) *The longest tee shots are those bullets that go in a straight line and roll forever.* FALSE. Unless you are playing the Bonneville Flats Yacht and Country Club. A golf ball is sitting on a tee minding its own business. Along comes a mass, propelling it off into space; the ball is moved by force, and because its surface is not smooth, aerodynamics come into play. It will

reach maximum distance when the combination of force and spin work together.

If the trajectory is flat, the ball looks like it falls out of the sky. This is force without enough spin. If the ball starts out flat but climbs vertically into the sky, then spin has taken over and is not in synch with force. If the ball rises in a rocket-like trajectory, reaches an apex, and falls to earth, it is the optimum combination of force and spin. Buy the club that produces that shape. What is the optimum trajectory? That's a tough call. I've seen flatter drives run out, and later the same flat trajectory doesn't carry a rise in the fairway. My best answer is that every long hitter I've seen launches the ball.

(11) *Softer shafts and softer golf balls work best for most golfers.* TRUE. Yet why do I see so many golfers playing golf balls especially designed for faster swing speeds? The application of softer shafts has been written about many times in recent years and I think the public is getting the message. Remember, the job of the shaft is to help you return the club head to the ball in a square position. The shaft doesn't create energy, so find what works for you.

One of the greatest changes in modern golf is our ability to try golf ball designs until we find one that fits our game. In the old days the biggest variable was the brand and the number on the ball. There were ultra-wound balls for the elite player or the wealthy, because they'd cut if you looked at them funny. I haven't seen a smile on a ball in years, but I do see folks playing with expensive brand-name balls that don't fit their swing speeds. I don't know if it's ego or great branding. Don't be afraid to experiment—you'll be pleasantly surprised.

(12) *Custom-fit clubs will cause you to swing better.* TRUE. I've seen this firsthand and it surprised me. After I thought about it for a while, it shouldn't have; it is relatively simple. One

of the keys in a custom set is good posture, both at address and during the swing. Combine that with the proper club length, shaft flex, and lie, and a custom set is there to do its job. The primary objective is to decrease your bad hits and increase the probability of good ones. Once that process starts, your personal computer recognizes what is going on and Mr. Confidence enters the picture. It doesn't take much time as the parts of the process work together, and you in turn will make better swings. Am I a proponent of custom clubs? You bet I am.

(13) This last question is a multiple choice: You enter a golf shop where the professional has been granted magic powers. He can grant you one golf wish. You get to improve your game, and make it more like that of a tour player. There are four choices: A) longer, straighter tee shots; B) longer, accurate second shots, say, from 160 yards to more than 200; C) more accurate short shots including wedges and chipping; or D) better putting. Whatever the degree of improvement, it will be the same in each category, so to move your game closer to that of the touring professional, you get to pick one, which will produce the best result. You in this case are an avid golfer, say a bit better than average, a sixteen handicap.

A _____ **B** _____ **C** _____ **D** _____

The answer is B, the long second shot. I'll now allow five full minutes for the putting crowd to yell at me and explain that putting is half the game and that even a minor improvement in putting will show up in the score.

Now imagine that you are playing in a scramble, one of those events with A, B, C, and D players, and the handicaps are fair. The A player has just hit a big tee shot and your team is facing a 192-yard forced carry over water to the green. Truthfully, how many guys need to get out of the cart besides the A player? The answer is maybe the B player, three times out of ten. The A player hits a nice shot onto the green eighteen feet from the cup. Now how many players are in the game? How many times has the D player been the best or at least tied for the best putter?

The answer is letter B, the second choice, because for a long second shot to a green, most of us play to some degree of failure. Sure, we don't putt like the pros, but sometimes we come close. Yet we very seldom hit high, long second shots softly onto the green. If we want to score more like the pros do, we need to improve in that area.

In seminars I'll inevitably get someone who says my answer is wrong. They have the putting yips, or they can't get off the tee, and those are the areas that need the genie. They're absolutely correct, but my question is of a general nature. Just yesterday I was watching a tour event on TV, and the leader missed two putts under four feet on the back nine; he also hit a beautiful four iron 227 yards over a hazard onto a green. I can make a four-foot putt; under those conditions I might have choked so bad that I'd have three-putted, but I *can* make a four-foot putt. Put me a 227-yard carry over a hazard and, unless I bounce off a turtle, it isn't going to happen. That tour player has a full shot advantage; from 227 I'll always be laying up, but at 197 if I improve and can get my ball on the green or fringe, my scores will go down.

I could start playing 6,000-yard courses where my second shots never exceed 147 yards. But I'm not that smart and don't have control over my ego.

THIRTY-THREE

THE SECRET OF GOLF

*I*n the first place, let me definitely state that there is no one secret to golf. That's why hundreds of books have been written on the subject. It's just a catchy chapter title to hold your interest as we get to the end. If anyone tells you they absolutely have the secret to golf, you should proceed carefully, very carefully. What follows comes from thirty years of experience, not just as a fellow golfer but as someone dedicated to making products that help golfers play better. Beyond just observation, I've had the opportunity to make product, introduce it into golfers' hands, and watch the results. Moreover, as a watcher I reverted back to my old (very old) days as a field engineer. There, the use of statistical analysis was a tool to determine cause/effect in the application of my company's products. In other words, the watching wasn't casual and, despite my disclaimer about secrets, this chapter will help a lot of golfers.

The old saying, "It makes no difference if you think you will or you won't, you're right," is on track, but it's too simple. I don't want you to *think* you will, I want you to *know* you will, and therein lies the challenge. I *know* I can hit a golf ball 160 yards over a water hazard, but I *think* I can hit one 180 yards over the same hazard. Those are two completely different mental environments, often leading to different swing efforts, and if I need to clarify the 180 yard swing is the ugly one.

When I was a club fitter I ran this test dozens of times, enough to prove my premise. After a fitting, if I had a little time, I'd ask the golfer if he minded assisting me in a little experiment. Being the genial folks golfers are, the answer was usually yes. I'd have four five irons and I'd say, "Would you please hit these while I record the data." (I used a very accurate electronic device.)

"Now, before you start," I'd tell them, "I don't want you to get frustrated, so I'll be clear that the first two irons are nowhere near your specs. I don't expect the shots to be good. The data is relative. The second two are very close to what you need, so ball flight will be better, but this experiment is about relative ball flight, not pristine shots." Why did I say this? Because I wanted them to understand that there was no pressure to perform. This was a data collection effort; I didn't want anyone frustrated by hitting poor shots with clubs that were specifically the opposite of what their specs required.

Although I didn't mention it, technically the test was flawed. I had identified the differences in what I was testing, and it should have been blind. As the test unfolded, without exception shots from the "wrong" clubs rated poorer than the "correct" ones, but after all it was just data collection. One thing I forgot to mention: I switched the clubs! They hit the wrong ones better than the right ones. Why? Was I a lousy fitter? Did I get the specs backward? No. Actually I was a good fitter. What happened was that for a brief period I was able to enter the psyche of the golfer. Custom-fitting creates a bond. If I take you to the range and demonstrate that I can improve your ball flight, I've earned a measure of your trust. I knew this, so my experiment was designed to create a mental image of ball flight relative to the clubs the golfer thought he was hitting. I wanted to see if this was more powerful than the clubs themselves.

An easy answer is to write all of this off to inconsistency, and I've heard that hundreds of times. "Barney, it's my swing, I'm so inconsistent." Yes, all golfers have inconsistencies, but when you take data, it's surprising to find that the inconsistencies tend to repeat, and that means as a fitter I can help. Take this example, one that every golfer has experienced. You play three or four holes well, hitting good shots, and the definition of "good" here is relative. "Good" for a low handicapper isn't the same as for, say, a fifteen, and I'm talking about shot quality. Then a demon invades your body, and for two holes the shots you hit resemble nothing you did previously. Is this simply the inconsistency of any golfer defined by shot variation? Did you get to a state of mental discomfort? Golf holes that intimidated? What happened? You weren't under huge pressure, you truly thought the shots were going to be as planned, but something happened. I believe there is a fundamental technical error most amateurs make that leads to this condition, and when it happens it undermines our relatively fragile confidence resulting in poor outcomes.

When I worked the range I looked for and recorded characteristics of shot performance. I had electronic measuring capability, and working with tour-caliber players devised a test. I'd give them, as an example, a five iron, and say, "Hit it to that flag. It's 135 yards" (which it was). On the first swing the ball would hit near the flag. I repeated the experiment with different players, different yardages. Excellent players, tour-caliber, have wonderful distance control and it was immediate, meaning they accomplished the goal on the first swing. I tried this with full swings as well as shots that required manipulation, like the 130-yard five iron. (By the way, if you're an aspiring young player, a great way to practice is to go on the course and, instead of hitting each shot all out, try the 150-yard five iron to learn the feel of controlling distance. That's not the secret I refer to, but it's a very good tip.)

When I asked average golfers, say eight to eighteen handicaps, to do the same thing (the 135-yard five iron), invariably a different pattern developed. Shot one would be fat, and go nowhere. Shot two would airmail the target, and by shot three or four one would go near the requested distance. This was a phenomenon that repeated itself, and I filed away the data. Generally speaking the higher the handicap the more difficult this test—essentially a predictable result.

What I have learned: 1) the average player has poor distance control; 2) his mistake, especially in the longer clubs, is short; and 3) after enough swings, even the average player on the range achieves a relative form of distance control.

That is very good stuff. But why does it happen and how can I use the knowledge to improve ball flight? The answers reversed themselves in order. Golf is played one shot at a time (okay, duh). Good players had good distance control on the first swing, which is essentially real golf. The rest of us didn't. However, average golfers in practice would hit several shots with one club and somehow determine their capability, which they felt they could take to the course. Could I come up with a way to make this process more effective?

Finally, I figured it out, and like all such things it was really fairly simple. The average player hits his wedge, a nine iron, with relative consistency for distance. The extra loft, spin, and the shorter shaft all contribute. Given that most amateurs aren't going to spend time beating range balls, they extrapolate by adding ten yards for the loft difference in each club to come up with a number. The process of hitting balls is designed to justify that number, not validate it. This is not a casual statement. In my years as a fitter I asked everyone the same question: "How far do you hit your five iron?" Excepting the elite player, every golfer I tested had one thing in common. Under electronic testing, they hit shorter than announced. My question was why. These weren't stupid people. I understand the ego, but that wouldn't account for the degree of discrepancy I tested. There had to be another factor. It was efficiency. Adding ten yards per club assumes the same ball-striking efficiency throughout, but for us amateurs it doesn't happen.

The club designer will say that he can fix this problem with modern technology. My response is that he can help, yes, but fix it, no.

Try this approach, and let me warn you that it involves hitting a fair number of range balls. Hit ten balls with any club, let's say a six iron to start. If you aren't working with an electronic measuring device, then hit to a known distance and measure carry distance only.

Throw out the two longest and the two shortest, and average the rest. That's the yardage I advise you to play for that club. Go through the bag and repeat the experiment. Hitting ten balls per club is a lot, so take your time and don't shortcut yourself. Do it over two or three sessions if necessary.

The best method for this experiment is to record the data, and when you're done sit down and review the results away from the range. You'll find out your average distance for each club. You'll find some clubs you don't hit well enough to put into play. You'll find some that you hit surprisingly close to the same distances and you'll find big gaps. You will receive an education on you and your clubs.

Here's a normal reaction to this process, so let's get it on the record. "I did what you suggested, Barney, and the average for my six iron came to 153 yards. Now, you know that's ridiculous. I can hit a six iron 163 yards." My answer is that when you play against me I want you to hit every club the distance you think you can, but when you're my partner I want you to hit them what you do on average. Golfers are an interesting bunch. A shot thirty feet short of the pin is okay, but hit one thirty feet long and it's "too much club, nearly airmailed everything." I guess you could do what I really do when I practice. Years ago I could comfortably hit a six iron 170 to 175 yards. Now I spend hours on the range trying to recapture that distance, my lost youth. Nothing good happens, nothing I can take to the course. But someday...

Why are we doing this and what is the secret about? Go back to my earlier experiment on distance control as the hallmark of the elite golfer. You suffer from inconsistency; I just showed you a method of closing that gap, of playing more like an elite player. As you gain more control of your distance on the course you'll understand how to hit the ball on or close to the green more often, and that means better scores.

Here's a true story about how I once helped a golfer and made his game worse. He was older, couldn't hit the ball very far, and constantly complained about hitting a five wood where we hit medium irons. I decided to help and made him a driver that he hit a good fifteen yards farther. It ruined his game. He could hit that five wood with amazing distance control. I "helped" him by getting him closer to the green, and he was hitting clubs with much less consistency than the five wood. It was a long time ago. I finally fixed the other clubs, but learned a lesson I never forgot.

Elite players need a different approach. Hit your driver, then an iron. Repeat through the bag hitting the driver, and then every other club, one shot each. Write down the carry distances. Your objective is defining the distance gap between clubs. As an elite player, you hit the ball well, and each club has a range, depending on how you swing—either "muscling up" or "taking something off." We know that. This isn't about you; it's about your clubs. What does each deliver with a normal swing, simulating the one-shot environment of real golf?

This is bonus stuff. Since I admitted I helped the player mentioned above by increasing his distance off the tee, it's only fair that I do the same for any interested reader.

Given the technology involved in today's drivers and golf balls, let me impart knowledge that will allow you the best mix of both to pick up more distance. Get stronger, specifically defined as club head speed at impact. The driver and golf ball design pale in comparison to increased club head speed at impact. I don't care if you spend a thousand dollars at the most sophisticated fitting center optimizing your driver head, shaft, and a correlating golf ball; getting "golf stronger" is the best thing you can do. That can be defined as a more efficient swing for someone who already has the necessary strength, or it can mean a strengthening program. Don't ask me how; there are many programs available, designed by experts in the field. If you want to drive the ball longer and your club head speed at impact is 86 miles per hour, improving it to 95 miles per hour with the same driver and ball you now have, even if they aren't quite right, will produce those precious extra yards. You can fine-tune from there.

No better place to end than talking about more distance, which is every golfers dream. In fact I think I'll go work on mine.

EPILOGUE

I hope you enjoyed the read, and I also hope that those of you on the business side took away something of value. It's been fun reliving the story. I have often been asked if I'm proud of the status of Adams Golf in the industry. Certainly, I am. It's a company of well over one hundred employees, and is a good community citizen, producing excellent products.

Entrepreneurs by nature look for more projects, though, and I am no different. This book was an enormous task, not just because I chose to write it myself, but because I had to overcome my total ineptitude typing on, and attempting to understand, a computer. My wife Jackie served as an unpaid technical consultant, and I'll be eternally grateful to her for her assistance. Furthermore, she now understands that computers don't like me.

During the writing process I was able to use my contacts through golf to ask questions of some very successful people. I told them about the book and confessed that in the world of business advice I was worried about being simplistic. The universal response was twofold: more businesses suffer from basic, simple errors than some kind of grand malaise, and the best way to learn is by experiencing or observing mistakes. That advice mirrored my writing approach and gave me the confidence to finish the task.

I'll use this space for a personal tribute. I was privileged to work as a fundraiser for a Dallas-area charity known as the Ryan Foundation, founded to help Ryan Dant and other children suffering from MPS (mucopolysaccharidosis). In this book I referenced my tough times, and frankly some were very difficult. However, becoming associated with the Dant family and learning about the disease MPS taught me that far stronger people than I face far greater problems on a daily basis. Imagine the shock of being told that your infant child has an incurable disease that will end in a terribly painful death by the age of ten to twelve. Further, because it's a rare disease, there is no cure, and no research being done to find one. Start with that premise and end up with an organization that successfully finds the path to a treatment that saves lives. For whatever my minor contribution, I received immeasurable benefits in return.

ACKNOWLEDGMENTS

*T*his has absolutely been the most difficult section of the book to write. I'm terrified I'll forget someone from that very long list of people who helped me along the way. Some are easy to remember, like my wife, Jackie, who was always supportive, even in the bad times. Mary Beth Lacy, simply the best publicist in the golf industry, with whom I had the pleasure of working during my active years at Adams, is another.

Fernando (Nando) Alviar, who ran manufacturing during my active days at Adams. Marc Puglielli (Max's brother) has been with Adams Golf for several years and is instrumental to our success internationally. Special recognition goes to Cindy Herrington, our Vice President of Marketing. Cindy is my daughter, and in an effort not to show favoritism over the years she never caught a break from me. I'm very proud of her. I'm equally proud of my son, Eddie, our legal counsel. He has been the source of some excellent advice. And I can't forget my daughter Susan who has always made me laugh.

I'd like to thank Ann Neff, my longtime assistant, and let me add one more piece of advice here. Anyone in an executive position who does not have an assistant that serves as a "right arm" is working less efficiently than they should. Old industry friends like Faris McMullen, Charley Raudenbush, Tom Fazio, Spike Kelly, Hank Haney, Bob Bush, Kim Calhoun, Carol Mann, Nick Aquilino, Lee Trevino, and Jim Hardy also deserve recognition, as do lots of folks on the media side: golfing friends Jerry Tarde, Jim Nugent, Jim Auchenbach, Al Barkow, Lorne Rubenstein, and, of course, Jim Dodson, who sat in my house and encouraged me to write this book. Adam Barr—a fellow jazz buff—John Steinbreder, Jerry Potter, Mike Lupica, Cheryl Hall, Michael Jacobi, Kenny Bob Davis, and let me stop here. Over the years I was lucky to make many friends on the media side; I can't name them all, and I hope they understand. Thanks also to George Klaus, Roy Kitamura, Roger Tonnesen, Greg Sollers, Steve Adams (my brother), and Rick Urdhal, who together formed the first investment group that got me started. My good friend Don Hall, a fine golfer and advisor, but of greater importance as my source for long discussions on professional hockey. M. Emmet Walsh, the fine actor and Clarkson golf teammate long before metal woods. Charles Summerall, who sponsored me into Preston Trail and still suffers the consequences.

My editor, Mark Weinstein, did his best to turn me from an enthusiastic beginner to the author of a book with structure. I thank him for his help and applaud his professionalism. Subsequent to Mark's work I received the benefit of long hours by Jessie Shiers, the copy editor. To both Jessie and Mark: I know I am an amateur and it took extra effort from both of you to turn the book into its current readable condition. "Thank you" seems inadequate, but understand that it is a heartfelt acknowledgment.

I'm stopping here. I just went through my old Rolodex and my contacts list. I could literally name scores of people who helped me along the way, including over a hundred club pros and retail folks alone! No one makes the small company journey by himself. The golf industry is full of wonderful people and I have been blessed with friends at all levels. Thanks to all of you!

INDEX